To Patricia Coyle

Contents

Author's Note

This book includes the contents of seventeen separate publications which appeared between 1967 and 1996, together with two fugitive poems from that period, 'A Former Boiling' and 'Inaugural Address', which came to be printed for the first time in the magazine *One* (1980) and the anthology *A Various Art* (1987) respectively. With the exception of these latter pieces which are placed in their order of composition, the works are assembled in chronological order of publication. Where poems were subsumed into larger volumes they have been separated out, omitted from the later collection and returned to their status as separate publications. The collaborative work, *In One Side and Out the Other* (1970), is only partially represented through the inclusion of the poem 'Israel' written with Andrew Crozier. A few errors in transcription or in printing have been corrected and some further amendments have been made in the interests of consistency of presentation.

For their support and for the original publication of works collected here I would like to express my grateful thanks to Andrew Crozier; Tim Longville and Gordon Jackson; Wendy Mulford; Ian McKelvie; Hilary Lane; David Chaloner; Mark Francis, René Block and Sir Nicholas Serota; Geoff Ward; Michael Schmidt; Jean Crozier; Peter Riley; and Rod Mengham.

For the present publication I would like to express my grateful thanks to John Kinsella; Christopher Hamilton-Emery without whose commitment and care this book would not have been able to happen; and Maria Gilissen for her generous permission for the use of Marcel Broodthaers' *La Soupe de Daguerre*.

I would also like to take this opportunity to express my grateful thanks for support along the way to Charles Tomlinson; Jeremy Prynne; Peter Ackroyd; Bruce McLean and Paul Richards; John Russell Brown; Alexandra Pringle; Barry Flanagan; Tom Raworth; Val Raworth; and to the University of Keele; The Arts Council; the University of Sussex; and Anglia Polytechnic University.

Mmm . . . Ah Yes (1967)

Shades in a Conversation

1. *"I thought I saw N.T. Clear the other night."*

familiar face
wavering through
thickening vapour

tongue buried in
mouth's hole

2. *"Wasn't he up the same time as you?"*

face luminous
in empty corridors
the book

slipped from
his fingers,
pages flutter

sound & resound of footsteps
in the high vaulting

Cool Evening

Fugue
      tranquillo

key
after key

touched
            hesitation

on the old upright

while
            out the window
two elderly ladies
in straw hats
fitted jackets &
crape dresses
slack over
thin calves

step by

the summer hedgerow
stippled with white
cow parsley

Plane Tree

lamplight ascending through
masses of hand-shaped leaves

yellows
now some
now other pale
undersides
as they turn
in the current of air

in which the tree's spread wavers
like a reflection
on disturbed water.

On the Way Home

water from the afternoon rain
ripples down the
laneside & air
breathes through
the valley
detailed in
sunlight

a passing wheel has
pressed a rat to
the tarmac

rooks
            scatter over
the tip

no one about
the sewage farm as
usual the
long-armed sprinklers
rotate over the
filter tanks &

from the stile the
right of way
straggles upward over
the pasture all
burst with molehills

Chi è Questa Che Vien . . .

after Cavalcanti

Christ
when she opens
the door
every man
turns to look at
her, the light
definitely
trembles &
no more than
a wordless
breath
hints at
her each
rare virtue yet
no other woman
has such modesty
& I think so
highly of her
I daren't
picture the
outcome

6:00 p.m.

Oh, CALYPSO
CAFÉ ESPRESSO
Charlotte Street, Clifton
last of the old 50s bars
in this quarter

with your decor of plaster masks
as detached as
the faces of your clientele who
stare at them
& the red roughcast walls
sectioned by bamboo uprights

or through the window at
the evening streets,
the pale stone octagonal
of University Tower
discretely presiding over
the nearer facades of
ladies' dress shops.

O, Καλνψω
we're all waiting quietly here
in that interim
before night
really begins.

While Listening to 'Ah-leu-cha'

the edge of paulton might be
any other little place tonight,
& any hedgerow might be smudging
the demarcation
of any thistle-ruin'd field & sky
trailing misty clouds & smoke
from a couchfire, the
gawky elms &
cottages depressed
left side the rise,
nearer, the new
unmetalled road
gravel blocks clay
smothering topsoil.
But the light which has been glowing on a pole
in the sunken lane
sharpens to a star against
black foliage now the dusk
& horns of 'Ah-leu-cha'
impel it to the focus of the mind –
backwards the sound
trails indeed
as he walks away
seemingly playing forever,
the sound of a dead man, but
as startling a light as that
which makes us look up
years after its emission
from hydrogen long spent

Hengrove

Drowsing. The warm air
hums through grills,
monotonous
accompaniment
to a film
without
music or
dialogue,
shown on a
cinemascope
window – the
pale green
playing-field to
middle distance,
the slowly curving
perimeter
a line the
jumbled backs
stop at. Poor
definition
of the little
brick & tiled
houses with
tiny black
windows,
children's
drawings with
square stacks
perforating the
slow grey skies –
a few weak
elms, branches
suffusing
the lower skies
with delicate
red of

pointilliste
winter
buds. For cast,
a blot of a man
in the middle
of the green, painting
invisible marks
on the grass; & the
regular extras –
a couple of hundred gulls
two pitch lengths
away, like dashes
of slush
till one throws
open its wings
in a gesture
that might well be
taken for
despair

An Open Letter to Jim Workman, Landlord, at the Rose & Crown, Withy Mills, North Somerset

your lame foot & stick
suggest pain
carry your
trunk, head, arms
hands, the drink in
your hand, a glass
mug, pint, bringing
it to us

& if I brought you a poem
what would you do with it?
what would your hawk's nose,
your dry sniff, pulled down
corners of mouth,
mockery of Old Winsley,
scrounging his way, the way
you made him an iced birthday cake
of wood, set light to his hat

you might burn
my poem & yet

the way you know the way
foxes kill young cuckoos
in long grass, you
bait the sparrows to
a roll of wire to
shoot them all at
once sitting up late with
one candle in the henhouse to
see & shoot a
corn-stealing rat,

or your care for
your great

decorative
dahlias, the size of
a man's fist set on
shoulder-high stems,
some so purple
almost black &
bursts of red petals
curled & pointing like girls' tongues
away from the centre, the flower itself
an image you have made.

You showed me the
way to bud the
briars in June,
splicing with
raffia. Told me
dung burns the roots off
beans, to repair
the rung of a ladder with
pitchpine – "from the guys,
used to let down
the cages –
there's resin in it –
don't need no
creosote . . ."

You know the skyline without
looking at it, the rise of
the hills, the fall of
this valley,
this little Cam
taking its way through earth
since before
any of us, the fields
multiplying through
division by hedges, the
grasses green from
decomposition &

explosions of grey-green
trees in a wet May
against a grey
West Country sky,

the rain coming in over Mendip
from the Atlantic,
taken for granted, making
the grass grow taller, taking
what sustenance it can, as I,
happy with cider, yet
standing in the land
where once was sung 'that song of Lawes' –
neck craning in the driving wet &
listening hard – while
you Jim, can get it mostly
from the earth your
feet press on, your way

is a poem,
my way is a poem,

the poem has its way.

What Can You Do With a Bird Like That?

for Nick

>   on impulse, drinks
>   still in hand, the
>   door ajar, barn owls
>   croon cool &
>   skritch owls

the cups left on the wall in the lane,
>   drained, walking
>   the cold air
>   made a hole in
>   the membrane of the eyes –

Where's the nightingale

a north wind –
>   either he's gone
or he's huddled in the tree's
thickly-leaved branches,
unable to sing as before –

so the eyes involuntarily shut
after cider &
>   long hours of conversation.
The back-ribs chill
from the unstopped gap

Walking on the Downs Near Avon Gorge

Gaiety in a friend,
it's true to say
infectious –

Pete's ironic
polaroids &
fanged smile
shine – lively
& ingenious
intelligence
exploding
in a variety of
elbow-armed gestures,

happy buffoonery
over the grass, the
eager response of his girl –

but walking ahead
to a higher place
above the gorge I
get to where
to look out
over to grey
blocks, distant
spindles of cranes
at Avonmouth
& beyond that
the misty Severn,
Newport smoking, the
vague cloud-
like mass of the hills
of the Marches
blending with cloud,
the unseen Midlands to the East

the concrete proof of distance
reasserts itself.

A quick wind
cools the cheek.

You are
that far
away.

Flowering Shrub

Abutilon –

        the spreading
fragility
      of our love

made clear –

delicate
trails of
saffron wood

floating over

a framework of
upright canes &
slight stems

(snowflakes

wind-flicked from
parapet

interpose
eye &
figure –

green cord,
black hose
round shin
& ankle, the hem
the knees lift
to go
through snow –

The pale
green leaves
are still
in the gentle air
of the warm room,
each turns from its
petiole with
the curves of a
palm from its
wrist, spreads
into three
broad points

(kisses, nose to
chin, leaning over
the high back of my
kitchen chair
glints from
the naked bulb
dilate &
contract in
your hair
a willow cave,
sunglints,
my face
content –

The many
pink flowers,
exclamations
in that tender
discourse, not
unlike in
shape & colour
the open parts
of a woman

(lips to
lips fit
like palm
to hip,
such a
comfortable
ease of
focus, the
relaxation of
all these
parts through
one part
in each –

The whole
shrub

lives

in its
big red
flower
pot, base on
a white
dinner
plate,

the root

invisible

To Allen Ginsberg

O fecund imagination, oh tender reader
    when you say "vagina" it
is a part of the human organism
    not a surgical name nor
a drawing on a lavatory wall
    & "cock" – whoever
could be revolted by
    your love for men
loves no man, woman –
    & when you sing
the mantras, the underside of
    the cymbal, its dark concave
centre no bigger than
    a nipple fixes the eye in
its shining setting of
    brass, the focus of
sound ringling round the
    blonde light spinning the
outer passive surface
    each time the other obscured by
your brown fingers sounds it:
    "to awake the spirits" is one reason
we sing, & if we awake
    we will love one another
for what is worth loving in each of us.
    No need to stamp about
to be a man, that kind
    of proof is unrequired.
But to recognise one another's
    needs, not to impose
the will but to caress
    without force – one's need
to be alone, yet also to be
    human together, to be humane
by caring – you asked us
    whether we got wet in the rain,

what woke the children, whether
    we had breakfast too.
To let what is violence in us not
    cut, but flower
like the cartoon, you drew one
    growing from the skull's teeth
like a poem of some permanence
    surviving the gone tongue:
what critics call the violent imagery in
    your poems does not hurt us –
all the pain of that is in you,
    what we have done to you
inflict on one another –
    in your delicate ankles, your exposed eyes
& your violated stomach
    when it heaves up
rejecting the poisons with a
    man's retching roar
my whole diaphragm chest lungs
    heaves with it is
the rejection of all that is
    sickening in our nature.

The Lovers

can bring you back
from a northern trip
down lanes of beech leaves
shining, swollen with sap, curled
from the bud-sheaths to the city,
can make it possible for you to see
blossoming cherries & almonds
in quiet suburban gardens

Stop thinking
& see how they
do it, how she is
active towards him, care
in his face in-
stead of worry,
separate threads of hair
translucent with sunlight
swirling round her child's face –
but the pressure of thigh
in blue levis
strong breasts in a
blue sweater &
look, she is actually
sucking her thumb.

To a Young Art Student in London

Ah Paul, look out your window –
here too these small trees
                seem to have been
    leafless for years –
             The energy is occluded –
   Great effort is needed
      to walk across the vast grass
    yet people move
            & we cannot hear them

When there is a day like this with
no more ecstasy left outside, when it's after
Cézanne's high réalisation
when it seems there are no new songs to be made,
after the betrayal of all the rebellions, the shooting of
   Makhno –

Nothing moving on the suburban streets of every European
   city –

you can only be sure of your own pattern of the force,
   revealed in
meteorite storms of colour
figuring the space round
your own iris,
next year's buds
         hidden in
this year's plant, the tree's
roots growing
      where no eye can see

This year you talk approaching the speed of thought,
     energy charges
       detonate muscles
        in tongue's rhythmic motions –

I pray you
safeguard that surety
& never eke it away in little
life-weary shrugs.

Danny's Plaque

the colour of pennies

                            issued to
millions – o wives, mothers

the expenditure!

one each for all their dead
& one for Danny

on a blue runner
on the sideboard
as I remember it, in
a little well-carpentered varnished stand of deal
made specially for it by my father –
though like me you also never knew him –

child-uncle of my mother,
etherial figure in her tale on leave,
unwinding & rewinding puttees
like a mummy's bandage so
unsolid in a child's thoughts' picture –
he dives like a noiseless gymnast
headfirst over the livingroom table
through the open window
into the backyard
& with fixed bayonet
pierces the inside of the front-door of the now demolished house
        in Roland Street

What I am allowed to say that I
know is – the papers – the edges of
pages of the diary,
charred with years-old blood

& a plaque for all the heroes.

But he is not a hero
in our family, but our poor Danny,
shot through the brains on the 10th of November 1918.

None of us ate them
in our family.

He informs me now
if only inasmuch as I am cells
proliferated from his mother – Granny:
great-grandmother. Hart.
Shadowy, black-clothed, white-haired &
many times bereaved lady of sorrows –

looking up at her, stirring
the best stew with dumplings
by the black range

Bathampton Morrismen at the Rose & Crown

The glossy saloons slide up the rise.
The dancers, faces oblivious & grave,
block them –

white cloth vibrating
against dark green hedgerow, the tiny bells sound a
fraction of a second before a leg is seen to move –
the heavy flesh leaps – thick thighs bring the hard heels down –

Hwaighh! – sticks clack on tarmac,
whap overhead.

When it comes, Renolds, with graceful nonchalant wrists
flicks his pair of handkerchiefs at a bass yell of thunder.
His soul flashes briefly in the white of an eyeball.

The solo dancer leaps,
straight & upright, chin hanging,
mouth of big broken teeth,
eyes rolling upwards in beatific idiocy,
looks into the interior of the heavens, the growling clouds
their innards exposed –
static explosions of rose & cream, Rose & Crown & roses still here
despite bombs in the 40s –
Jim leaning on his stick at the door
saw the limbs of trees
dislocate towards him –
a fast mass of air blasts atop the ridge,
goes clear over the roof of the house,
windows break in Timsbury
on the higher hill behind –

Renolds' sons dance too,
the smallest? – 8?
exactly following the five
men, advancing retreating,

stepping back up into the hedgebank
when pushed for space by his elders.

The saloons cannot get through.
Everybody ignores them –
they'll have to find their own gaps.

Strawberries & snails
sinking & rising
in my cidercup.

The Welsh Poems (1967)

Exultation

after Hywel ap Owain Gwynedd

A ton of white rain will overflow my self-shaped sleeping-bag of
    earth.
But today I love what is betrayed
by indifferent Saeson –
what will be obliterated
from the human view –

                     the curving horizon breathes
over the reclined anatomy of the sphere,
the open lands to the North & West
still sprawl under the windy skies beyond the cities –

& remote mountain plateaus –
                    Eglwysilan
where the shepherd raised his eyebrow
at the question put in English –

The waters of the Taff shine with the blackness of coal.
She gushes like piss
from under a mare's tail
out of the irregular
gap in the mountains, through the Vale
the low parklands barely embank her,
everywhichway discharging herself in
deflected forces of current
over the hidden rocks & the
spewing over at Blackweir
with a smell of dead chub & pit effluent.

The waves ceaselessly lay stress on the shore.

I love all wild rocky beaches –
the smashed boulders under the cliff at Marcross
& the calm pools left behind by the tide,

the smooth grey pebbles as big around as a cricket ball

& the vales & the wailing gulls
& the trailing-haired girls
& even fake Castell Coch with its phoney pinnacles, Disneylike in
      its half-shroud of dark beech woods

I care for the colliers, squatting on their haunches
on the swept pavements
under the shining windows
– Oh man, how bravely they bear up their spirits under the dark
      stress of the looming slagheaps –

But ach a fi, I do not care for the oppressive household
& war maintained in the interests of an economy.
I do not care for the offensive sight of uniformed spirits & I
      regret
the flashing of leather I made
in the mean alleys back of Charles Street
under the skies' dim glow from the foundries

A ton of wintery rain will overwhelm my lichened bed.

A ton of ocean, wicked with dread,
the colour of hoar-frost in its night of coming
curls over us.

Oh man, how far Worcester is from Newcastle –
we drove hard night & day to reach it.

O Earth, give me before my last lonely bed the love of her I love –

Duw! I take off in her élite beauty! –
Though my flesh carry a dark hurt in heart
may I find peace in my last nothingness –

A dark wave hangs over us

[34]

Second Exultation

after Hywel ap Owain Gwynedd

A broad band of hair
curls over the throat
like a fabulous gold collar
in lamplight, under it
un camée, l'oreille – a
hurt kissing for the
touch of frost,
a hushed parting.

& when she returned, sun-tanned, from the arms of The South
I fell to her again like a moth to the torch.

Though there was a girl who held back from
an eyed nipple & a nippled eye, for want of
the gift of a gold band,
holding my striped jacket tight about her –

& Gwyneth ducky, rocking her randy limbs
under mine all evening, a
gift on a plate, a brown-eyed mystery
whom I never had –
though I be done for slander, it grieves me
to hear of that healthy chick
wife to a briefcase –

oh but the white glare under black hair
                              of Lleucu laughing over
                              cider in the Dragon

my little finger
laid in the crease of her thigh & belly
under the table –
Her husband won't laugh if he hears this

[35]

& once I had a girl whose intention was as my own – to fuck & be
    done with.
I had a second – may they both be loved the more for that –
I met a third & fourth & got it –
I had a fifth who did not hesitate to slip down her odorous
    peccadilloes –
I had a sixth, ravishing in her white nudity, a bright girl who
    made a soft comfort from her dark hair –
I had seven & a severe strain. – Well

I accept involvement in the troubles that dog me,
& ah, my long-loved lady, desire
& the sweat of passion, alas are
natural to our suffering, my
elusive one –

come back from
that seductive sunshine

Heredity

following my father
through the echoing hall, the high glazed roof
& old galleries humming with
rock doves

I had not remembered so many cockle-stalls –
   the rattling of saucers swelling
   to a chattering
   threat of sound –

   the faded light
   mingles with the
   smell of sawdust
   & boiled shellfish

My father
dodging ahead
amongst the crowd.
A ragged-arsed urchin.

My father.
My father runs
naked across Kingsway, dripping from the canal
clothes under arm,
side-stepping drayhorses,
pursued by an old-time Cardiff cop –

my father hurls stolen eggs at the startled shavees in the Hayes
   Road barber-shop –

my father's fingers, crushed between tunnel & longboat,
bleed in The Royal Infirmary,

my father pelts
round the corner, collides
with crone

from the outdoor

jug shatters
on skull –

the amber drops still
fall in arcing splatters
in this room –

Following my father

straight check back of his retreating sports jacket
lost in a dark entry

Trägheit (1968)

The branches of the pine trees drooped heavily in the moist air. Grey clouds travelled in the sky, but all was so dense – and then the mist rose like steam, slow and clammy, climbed through the shrubs, so lazy, so awkward. Indifferently he moved on; the way did not matter to him, up or down. He felt no tiredness, only sometimes it struck him as unpleasant that he could not walk on his head.

At first there was an urge, a movement inside him, when the stones and rocks bounded away, when the grey forest shook itself beneath him and the mist now blurred its outlines, now half unveiled the trees' gigantic limbs; there was an urge, a movement inside him, he looked for something, as though for lost dreams, but found nothing.

GEORG BÜCHNER

Blues & Reverie

                    Eave-drops
spatter the leaves
                    in the darkness outside.

Really the end of another summer
you might say, & very little to show for it –
nothing for it but to tune to some distant crackly blues, take
        some light beer
mild cheese & pickles, feet up –

But the nagging persistence of the rain –
standing in it, with no visible environment,
hair sodden, water trickling
into ears mouth eyes, seeping in between the crevices – oh that
        future largesse of space
it will have to run through –

flesh swells then
falls apart like a kicked toadstool –

man's vague outline a
darker shadow in the soil,
spilled heap of cells,
conceding maze for wet to
infiltrate

pebbles shifting down, handful below handful
deep foot after foot in layers on the beach,
yielding to the wave & the
pressure of the water in its mass,

the grey brine where a surmised mind floats
submerged, looking up as if with eyes &
seeing beyond a shaken film of little breathing waves
a globe of light that swings down slow to
touch & test how air becomes

water, water air, – a difference
evaporates to mist
before the light's approach, embodiment
of down-air-stepping girl, hair
swinging from hairline, light &
sinuous as riverweeds fly with
the current . . . mmh, & her upwhisked
veily dress reveals then hides
then shows again, as if
the veils themselves were spirit
feebly striving for
embodiment, glimpses of
sunny limbs & free
uncluttered living breasts.
Before her as she moves a radiant heat
extinguishes the mist: attracts, absorbs
the whirling smokes. Steam becomes breathable air.
She takes my hand & leads me to a
shadowed room, a wall of which
is spanned with glass that shows the stars as bright & close as if
      the cottage edged upon a flat earth's precipice, beyond
          which
nothing but the endless drifts of space & scattered galaxies &
      nebulae.

The stars make the room seem cold.
Faint slumbery breath is picked up from the tumbled bed & the
      brittle light dwindles to
opaque air, to seething particles of dark above the bed.

I unbuckle my belt & lie down gently next my sleeping wife.

Runic

Now with so many years
& so much more that parts us
& you never write, do
you ever remember
how tenderly you bathed my face
that night I'd had a kicking
from the Southmead mob?

In the moonlit room
a tear dropped like a
transparent bead
into the pudding basin
your throat gulped
as we kissed,

I left dried scars of blood on
your soft coat

There can be no end to love begun in
such unglamorous
circumstances

A Dream

The travelling bookman will not sell his wares. He smiles.
– I only take he says –

you can touch & look but
not possess or read

He has a particularly attractive Keats, a
refinement of the tooled & gilted linen of Moxon's popular
      editions –

    The snot-green death-mask glows with a luminescence
        brief as a sparking meteorite in the dark temple of
          December skies/

  my father's face
  smiles sweetly as
  when younger:

  – What does it matter? Leave it – my
  thin clouds of glory are
  long spent – such puffs
  zoom off to
  nothing – vanishing dots
  on horizon –

    Walks ahead
    to the door

Variations from the Same Cramped Postcard

1

Dare I open my mouth to say
anything at all? If the lips become
ever so slightly full a
terrible roar like Frank O'Ryan's straight
from MacAlpine's Thursday & pay-night it
tears its loud way out into the jostling world,
the pent-up force of a swimmer's breath whose
stay beneath the waves has been too long
enforced, it breaks the juke-box
amplifier's limit.
Rather let me not touch the paper at all, lest it
scorch yellow flame weakly & gutter out.

2

I dared not touch the keys for weeks.
Fear of Lautréamont's sharks kept me away, the
black fins sailing the water
in little nervous curves. A
thunderous May & June, thick-aired summer
looming all evening over the suburban roofs,
distantly haunted by spidery tendrils of
bunched lightning. The rattle & smash of
thunder & hail on the roof are
indistinguishable. Of whom am I afraid I ask
myself in the glass? Were I to put down the razor
to one side, is there someone, who,
noiselessly stepping, would raise it behind me?

3

Responsibility overwhelms me. I put it off for days.
When the quiet morning finally arrives I know –
excuses have run out, it must be done at last.
Nervously hungry, I start
buttering bread & frying eggs.
I dust the typewriter, shuffle the packs of
disordered books, searching for lost paper.
Works by men who've squandered less pop out at me
like Zebadee on his spring.
But I must urinate, cut my nails –
Will the real work of poetry ever have such refining effects?

Days Passing

We stand talking in the parks.
Battered wallflowers. The cold gale blows
the grooming out of our hair, our coats
flap about us, are almost detached from
any place around our bodies.
Spectacles are opaque with raindrops.
Lunch-time shoppers jostle us
but we ignore that distant faint ripple
as our eyes, moved by the cortex, dream the words we
gesticulate into emphasis,
pounding along for miles.
The after-lunch conversation curves with the ease of a single
        sentence into night. We make poems.
The fabric of York Minster shifts very slightly.
Particles, suspended in the rivers,
flow very slowly out to sea.

Inventory

Whichever way I get there, driving or walking, Bristol or
Ely, the tawny fenlands
withdraw to the hem of
the sky, the passing of the afternoon
fails to bring any new thing near to hand, so the
whole flat range of the tenuous
ground seems on the point of
disappearing. Or to that large city
or any other where a man might go, desirous
of a beloved citizen, or to regain the
ease long-practised in that
known yet coveted place, when,
in the last miles, the hills, rain-dark & green,
all softened over at their tops with cloud, stimulate
irritation rather than affection, so eagerly
are we mindful of where we want to be
beyond them. Neither does the cathedral & its
awful insolence. Its shining roofs keep
shouldering off what scanty trees
there are, yet jealously withhold
the satisfaction of that nave for those
already close up under it, the priests.
Nor is it the elation there is in the sunlit
curvaceous chromium rippling &
whiteness of towers, the city, approaching from
the high road, entering from Wells, before you
slide down into her. Nor is it
the burn of ripped blisters or the
chafing of knapsack straps. Nor the cramped knee
under the column or the daze of thought in that
continued & distracting movement, the road a
swarm of gravelly microbes endlessly approaching
the flying outstretched wing.
                    Whichever way I go,
what aches frets stirs or elates, continually recurs,
& has its own self-consciousness. It is like

what we want least to be
deprived of. We hold on hard
to the being able for it, like to the wall of a cliff,
the embrace that none would want to fall
away from. Having known it; or about to.
Having said goodbye, or having no need to. Or
hello.
                    I kiss the palped tongue &
glassy teeth. They prickle with
the aroma of crushed cloves. Sometimes.
It remains like an undispellable lost dream,
preserved in aspic or the place
that lacks it. But I desire a tongue
not distanced from its proper closeness to the feeling brain,
no experimental snail's heart
pumping on a weighted string. That
only lived two days unnaturally preserved.
I would speak out not in solution, but cell to cell
as long as I remain unsevered from my purpose.

The Small Henderson Room (1969)

. . . or as we wheel
down over Crickley, chivalrously high on our seats
        you see across the gleaming generous screen
  right to the Severn Valley, tawny with the broad
        spread of distant grain, & beyond
        is where I'm going, where the mountains
        put up their profiles &, in the moister
        air of that higher altitude, the woods & valleys
        will be deeply soft & made greenly
        vivacious again.
                    In a mutual presence
        catastrophe may be averted, &,
        for myself, new paths of motion are asserted
        out of that & the gentleness a lady does
        grace me with. So I relax,
        sustained by a net of neurones like a hammock
        which we cause to dance
        & we are regenerated by it &
        the soft flicker of myoclonic light
        just under the skin. The paroxysm of an embrace is
        the intense & complete awareness of one
        another as dream for example – either you are my sister
        or my brother, or I have known you all my life.
        It is the amygdala that gives me being as
        an imagined creature & after your remaking
        the first thing you do is call my name. – Thus we
        recall the moment before, both what
        happened to us & what we did
        as from the tops of small hills
        blackness is eased away
        under the green & delicate
        leaves of the border hardwoods. They
        do not separate from the grey skies
        flashing with intermittent sun. It is we who are
        threatened by the children of empire at Burrium,
        but the Olway is fluid enough to be ours

& the ease of your disposition towards the world
can be & is as lovely as that – we remember; & so
we are aware of ourselves as persons with a
particular history – the circuit
touched off by everything we see or hear
appraise & want to do.

With Regard the Matter of Falling

A slight sense of the necessity of movement
wafts us forward through the
lilac undertones of twisting lane, field & hedgerow, weights
such as baskets
drop from our disinterested fingers
in this shared brief absence from such traffic
as passes.
              Her tall waisted figure
supports the head, the centre of all
imagination's longing, out of which the lifeful
hair is nourished by
the mallow underglow of circulation, a transient
fine pulsing, a degree of complexity
engendered in the natural self. What most fits us,
like a headscarf say, can be left
behind the arc of a wrist in air & be
retrieved from that current again as if
never let slip. Like when an interlude
imposes on rare & totally
engrossing liveliness of discourse
it is natural to run to it
to begin again.
              Already the skin trembles
with predisposition & there
is the cry, the small & rounded
mouth, the final ideogram of a call to aid &
contact for which I am more than ready.
I hear it with my eyes, despite the
rattle of drills & subterranean
booming of television speakers & all
those other whinings for attention.
The arms are raised, the hands
above the head are open, a
submission to the potential that
must strongly stride to it, that gesture, a
turning from the top-step of the altar that puts

the aimless athletic ritual of the priests of
false holiness to shame for ever.
It is the body of one being given up with awful
risk to the humanity of another – total
belief in the possibility of what we
must have & use, & that includes
such a degree of separation that
we will never be able to detach ourselves
from the knowledge of shock
& motion which is a blue light in
the hands as, with what we can of slowness, we
hold on to them, as the other leans
back to their bed of clay. That
is our only obligation, to prevent
all possible injury. We have only ourselves
to ease the rigour of our
hurtling impact with the
indifferent tarmac. The obliterating roar of jacks
pulls at our shifting glance but
finally, who else to lift us, as I have just
offered you my right arm & you can take it
still as we go to rest near
the gate of a quieter field.

On Leaving the Footpath

The metal of the footpath is
narrow & confined, its walk
short & crooked round
the hideous hangars. But
pausing for an hour or two
resting on corn stubble, that
glossy yielded ripeness
really does take on its curved
quality of extension from us as we
push it out in a wide
hillock-shaped surface, catching
the sun on its skin with the
same aplomb of intention there is
in the cup of a radio telescope. Alive
we hold it all, the signals
separately received are
poised in balance by the achieved
leap we are & the fence of
the footpath is oh a
hundred yards away, warded off
with the same intuited use of magic
or selection that the
corn too has used to give itself
significance & its own chance of survival.

Written on Beginning Georg Büchner's *Lenz* & While Waiting a Return

Lost on the outer rim of some
barely perceptible whirling, I float
slowly in toward the other. It is
no longer necessary to look for
lost dreams, the dream is found &
has a tangible & purposeful
content. A hillside breeze
ruffles the hair about
the temples in it. We know it
is a dream we have called into
being of necessity; &, with the joy there is
in returning to a friend or
place we have long craved
to be with or at, we look in
at each other, as though from a
long way off. But the void is
cancelled by our own assertion:
the codings of our senses fuse
into created fulness the apparent
immovability of the clouds as they
caress the turbulence of these hillocks &
valleys, ours, as far as the eye can reach.

Poem of Inevitable September, or, I'm a City Boy at Heart

The well-known details of the impending season
are all quite obviously real, though I'm not sure if
we're in the restaurant or on board a
Conrad Aiken liner or a Black & White bus, so I look
down through the characters on the window
at the street instead, but it's certainly not
water nor moving, but muddily dark with
neon red & orange stupid traceries to emphasise
the gloom, though it can't be much after eight, &,
of course, we're not on a Conrad Aiken liner but
looking down out of quite another sort of emptiness
into an English thoroughfare, in a town so small you can
feel it all day like wearing a collar
a size too small & it must be Tuesday night or something
for there's no one walking there. In the evening
the river bank is inhabited by a cold wind that
sneaks out of the bushes & touches its
palms to the small of your back for an instant, a
middle-aged queer who'll never admit to his own
propensities. Maybe we have just realised
it's all more difficult than we'd allowed for
basking in each other's vigour & the sun's, a
couple of repleted cats, but we aren't
cats, & I refuse to eat all that badly cooked rice:
what I make of the situation is what I make of the situation.
Every place you go they mourn the gone
pleasure of the summer, wondering if all their friends
have moved to another town. We're all
very seriously in debt to one another, but that's
more reason for not allowing a change of season
coax me out of what I go on thinking
despite it. I have desire safe against the mist here,
locked in its box of bone. I look into you again &
know we can still find ourselves out on the street
walking very slowly towards the taxi
not at all cold. We have at least another two hours.

"Whatever You've Got, Someone Somewhere Needs it" – W.M.

Fresh bread can taste so good, it's so rare
we eat it together. But it's hard not to see
outside in the rain, the winking
taxis, their swirling continuum into
the Circus. There has to be some way of stopping
that secret ticking of meters or else
allow ourselves to be towed
into the same winking connivance at
all those miserable buildings & the means for which
each single brick was put there, filling the space so
emptily at night in this great
city of the homeless. The clothes
on our own particular backs may not be
threadbare yet, but why should that distract me from
the reasons why I have the debts I do.
I can't stop such misery even as I see
spread whitening her face now that
the business of return has gorged back up
our limited allowance. Someone somewhere is
opening an oyster with a vicious
intensity of greed to have
the parts apart. As casually as that
blood can be washed away from the heart by a mere
application of property. A projectile, or even a
prior claim on paper. The dead guerilla's face
smiles up at us, eyes open. Maybe we can
arrange something out of it – you manage to step
out of the car, I manage to stay in the car &
drive with reckless speed for home. That
charisma, his & yours, confronts me all day long.

Waiting

So here I am in Martin's bathroom; what am I
doing in Martin's bathroom? It's simply that
I've used a lot of different bathrooms lately,
the point being, as usual, I'm desperate to be
somewhere else. But also as usual there's never
leeway enough of situation to
exercise choice. Too bad that isn't the name of
my pet dog then I could call it
to heel. But it must be true I haven't such a thing
for even my laziest acquaintances
call me desperado. Anyway,
it's a good clean large white
bathroom, with little bottles of TCP &
patent medicines for improving the health of
the teeth. I pull all the strings
that dangle provocatively reminding you
of the transient nature of things, which is to say that
these small furnished flats are common in
the semi-suburbs of this tiny academic town
& they are rented out by numerous
semi-professional landladies, who, of course,
live on the premises, whereas I'm just
looking thankyou in the pantry. There's some cheese
of a standard English variety & I break off a chunk &
eat it, grimace, decide to save the orange juice
for later, conserve the energy it would take to
wash the dishes left from lunch, go back &
flop out by the gasfire. I glance from
spine to spine of all the books I've never read:
they're there, around the walls, Engels &
Merleau-Ponty &, Christ almighty, I should have
read that, Jack London's *People of the Abyss*. I will.

Soon. Meanwhile I've developed a neurasthenia of inaction. I
   can't
bring myself to go on with that. But I would like some Prokofiev
& therefore settle for Barshai's orchestration of
Visions Fugitives. Immediately it's 9:25 & fantastic.

2

Here the workers are wearing it as easily as
their second-best suits. Their faces shine
from the effects of weather & soap,
their eyes are puffed as though with
Stelazine & the guards have shadowed bands
across their brows. Perhaps it's the new Hammer Production
Transylvanian policemen's hats. What is
the executive of the NUR doing? I haven't read
today's instalment, the bloody
mary tastes like piss as I expected, the barmaid
who is excitingly crosseyed is
exclusively fascinated by her future
domestic partner sitting across from her
with his cigarette, they have another
cigarette, but meantime we're all without a drink as
the juke-box plays The Secondary Sexual
Characteristics of a Whole Generation. The Calendar
Girl is wearing a voluminous skirt, but she has pulled it
up over one pinkly uninteresting
leg & is pointing to her
suspender. She has a smile on her face.
I think she's going to give herself
an enema.

3

The waiting room is certainly
warm enough to make it understandable
why people forget they are waiting.
But the platform is almost intolerable –
cold & dark, yes, but also motionless enough
to be a halt, not a station. It's so
solidly unreal – can it ever receive
a train from The City?

4

The newly ploughed field was once a place the lady & I could
lay down graciously together. The back rests of bales
are all gone. The precise gradations
of the season are all gone. The gentler aspect,
its last brave pimpernels & daisies & so many other
inconspicuous flowers that in her absence I can't name
have gone too. I carefully watched the leaves lose self-
determination in the sound of their own slow panic
in the south-west wind, warm enough that to
stand out in. They couldn't
be leaves, they sounded so like a mill-race
near-at-hand, till they ripped
crisply off, clipping the faces of passing cyclists.
I was glad. I wanted it all. To go. The trees
were soon burning all right. I didn't begrudge them.
Now the branches are the colour of wet slagheaps.

5

In a new blue room I rearrange
the mantelpiece, opening on it
the catalogue of the *Survey '67* exhibition at Peter Cartwright's
Three. Those anonymous forms wait, shakily
menacing to change shape, making
a new & unpredictable arrangement
of themselves. "Any references in my work are oblique
and are references to mood." Paul Wallace could be
writing of these paintings. Why not? Will his new magazine be
flashily shining in metallic folders & glamorous
with risqué visual material? I feel in need of
some elegant vulgarity in all this
Anglian smog that tires the eyes
till they smart. & John & Pete &
John? It doesn't matter who. At least
at the concert it's just about possible to
disregard so many empty seats & the
names that could fill them.
Under a cloudless permeable canopy there are
harp solos more brittle & glittering than silver
paper smoothed by a child's fingernail.
But why, between fast-driving departures to the city for high
        adventure
these cultivated silences? I'm tired of
all that posturing busyness
exclusive to all else.
Gill Vickers is walking very fast out of the station portico
        carrying a suitcase containing a large file of poems written
            while on remand, &
Merlin is already walking up & down outside his cave & looking
        at his watch.

6

(letter)

Doch reiner ist nicht der Schatten
der Nacht mit den Sternen,
wenn ich so sagen könnte, als der Mensch.
& you whether wearing
the myrtles of Greece or whatever
other corrupted soil or country,
lady & all who are named
ein Bild der Gottheit surely
the Colonels cannot continue
indefinite cheesecloth of
hazy newsreel uniform
or the recollection of a stout voice
familiar from childhood, repeating
over a hidden speaker: "a more
realistic level of unemployment in certain
selected areas" in certain selected
areas where you are so close to now
the harshest most expensive days come
inexorably in to many & that valley where we,
uneasy as strangers (star-rangers) saw them
float, lost in the eye of the hopeless
calm remaining after the withdrawal
of the stormiest fringe of the
anti-cyclone. An ultra-temporary system
of careless hand-me-down employment,
& as the trees fell all along the valley,
their fathers' fathers were sucked
in, migrants from scatterings of other
ultra-temporary arrangements that failed
finally, as this one does, expectedly,
as they might have. We climb up & out of it &
look down to the Ryan's plant, agitated
wasps, eating the coyly indifferent
encrustations in the valley.

That was almost a full half-year ago & they still wait for work.
A few more lines & I'll go & wash a shirt or my hair or my body
& that'll refresh my person, its sweat will flow away.
An easy self-refinement. Or I'll go down
to the huge brown hall & its empty chilling air & try
a phone-call to another vigilant in this
neighbourhood. I will look up from that
to the discoloured ceilings & the dust'll be
drifting down across the waning light from outside,
& the unkempt floors & tired walls will keep
very still & quiet while I'm waiting.
Wie ist mir's aber, gedenk' ich deiner jezt?

Coda to the Immediately Preceding Poems

& then we arrive hand in hand at
the raft-like railway terminal
which is really the deep-blue hangover
from the winter solstice as they play
Webern's *Opus 7* 1910 for violin &
piano over the tannoy system
instead of announcing the trains & I'm glad
we still have all the Berlioz
somewhere in the boot as I digest
my beautifully tenderised (by you)
& slow-cooked casserole of steak
I slowly uncoil from weariness
like an about to be transmogrified
boa-constrictor & I'm happy
to reassure you when you're frightened
by the reverend black lieutenant
rising on silent bicycling feet the
staircase as we overtake the taxi,
smoothly, because of our new improved
silencer. How can the nobly tall
look fragile as an ice-skater?
There's a delicate broderie Anglaise
hem to everything in this maturely
dignified tree-house.

Side Window

What trees are those, where the low clouds infiltrate
the furthest limits of the fen? We may discover,
sooner or later, should we venture out across
the languid fields. Meanwhile, my position lacks sense –
I'm neither perturbed nor unperturbed. As long as
I know it's either raining or not raining, what can I
know about the weather? That's not to say
there's no place to begin, but you hesitate,
wary of possibility b: a couple of arrows
departing in opposed directions. Thus,
the contemplative delay cannot be named
indolence; rather a poised inhalation of . . . er . . .
certain powers. But what a pleasure to clean
the petulantly dirty staircase & munch a
sandwich with you, standing at the sink, talking
over our plans as we let the afternoon
recline to its conclusion with as much poise as Manet's
Olympia, but not so bold erotic or passé – just
resting, calm in the assurance of a lack of stasis.

There is a very slight relief in
driving out of streaky pale cloud,
bordering trees, broad flat strips of
dead grass, crepuscularly edged
like bands of colour in
the pictures of that distant planet.
The mist was the most delicate of presences,
only discernible as droplets in
the separate waving hairs of the head,
& a large heron, lunging low away across the fen,
surprised the innocent eye which took it
for some great legendary bird
instead of the scavenging fish-eater
it really is. About the week-end streets
it is impossible to roam with any pleasure,
booted & muddy after the preceding walk,
& as I pull the wheel of the clumsy vehicle
slowly through the turn as the filter
invites me, a sad-lipped girl, who half averts
her head of profuse hair, lingers on
the kerb as I change up past her. How can I not
be touched by that as my son
touches with weightless fingers my
grey hair, Mélisande?

Forsythia spatters the faint loops &
twirls of vegetive nonentity with its own
forthright unconcern at being the primer of
this serial softening called days; even in untended gardens
& waste ground. Elsewhere we continue over
the dropped thorns & spiky shootings, wearing the strong but
flexible boots especially acquired
for dealing with such critical
impingements. From these we look to the floating bowls.
Are they fading to lighter vapours, or conspiring to
opaquer glowerings, more like the darker masses in
the chiaroscuro of our daily
moods?
   About the uncertain, we must be bold, sometimes,
like the closing passage of the *Satz*:
Beschwörungstanz in Henze's *Third*.
        My love, wonder & be
half-aware of an emerging freshness. It is about to
crack the umber of its bud while we go on to where
there is, delicately far, but insistently approachable,
an aspiration to a distant eminence.

A Public Self-address System

What a range of possible action:
        But we must, by necessity of essence,
be capable of holding up
      those modes unsuited to the moment –
there's a whole system of choices
by which to operate
& that's an intrinsic feature of you, butty!

So play something grand but schmaltzy like the
Siegfried idyll & I'll put on my old purple
& black bathrobe & stalk up & down
the crummy mat, trying to divert
the circular pathway of this brooding with thoughts of
Augustus & The Official Court Poets before we all
get involved in some boring literary argument
about spontaneous prose.
                  We are standing
on a smallish island off Europe – how horribly debilitating
that almost always has been. I'm too tired
to think of possible exceptions. But look out! Buzzards
don't get a feed without flying straight some of
the time. When the music stops you'll have to hear
the miserable whine of traffic in the streets.

This to be done
        before I do that, like
drinking the coffee before I can
    look into the morning
light. My brow feels caught inside
    a cap. But what is there
        to speak of else? Perhaps a
    lost delicacy at the
        faint lips might cause me
    tremble as do the uneasy
sycamores before the
        rain, turning their leaves
            pale underside o
            ver what delicacy I can
        not find, likewise my
            spectacles or a
                reason for

                        not keeping still I
                squirt the insects the trees
                        their metal leaves
                            uneasy go
                        into the harsher
                            light of dusk.

        The merest
        thing we are
            can often falter is
        utterly otherwise
        as often as
            not a
        fallen pen, no
            declaration to
            the summer if it start
        or draw the cork
            the wine may pour & it
        shine while we
            sleep, divining

& when I wake, please I
            walk in the
            sunflecked trees of
            the grove, for she herself
            may be felt to
            pass there,
        & her hand as a
            breath moves out
    on a tenuous
            breeze that lightens
        the ache. My shoulders
have learned to be
        tense in the night

Talking in Bed

Always it seems, the burbling trumpets
      wave you goodbye you wave me
      goodbye slow dawns before the film
       dispatches the rolling wheels of cars
      encouraged by harpsichords
Gently the rise is breasted
      you found the river the
  John Burns in dry dock for repairs
  an island with trees
  no traffic wardens where you were. ". . . Only
  24 hrs . . . & the spider brushed against
  your lovely adam's apple
  as it descends over your sleeping
  through Willis Conover & again
  in 1968 I'm left alone in sneezes
  under the dusty beeches Martin
  glimpsed through Collett's window
  steaming in his impossible green rain-cape. Impossible
  things French in English poems
  are so, well, stale, like an old *Paris Review*
  as it flops from your fingers goodnight

The Postcard Sonata

1

so, awkward lazy & indifferent,
I mooch along no tiredness left.
Under gigantic limbs of trees, the air's
persistent pressure cloys at
the skin as damp as steam & light,
tawny as amber, drools slowly by.
The whole flat range of the tenuous fens
may even trickle with it

over the horizon's precipice. If I continue
on my hands the pain I carry
in my legs may die, fading to nothing as
the scattered galaxies & nebulae
merge from their nascent places in the
endless drifts of evening sky.

2

for Andrew Crozier

Fluff, grit, various royal deceit de nos jours
began coming home to us in 1967 Andrew,
visiting the Borough gallery in Camden, eyes
blank with the dream of our cock-eyed dreams
the dawn thing suddenly isn't tenuous
admiring Peter Cartwright's *One Two Three
Four & Five* all menacingly fluid but
precise, a relationship between the formal

& the unpredictable. Later driving away
with a friend who'd deserted his wife
a journey of sickness on his sleeve,
they saw the outer lights of the city
a fabulous gold collar agleam
& liked those careful graduations also

FORTY

with Andrew Crozier

I walk along, left so alone,
indifferent, lazy, the gigantic limbs
of awkward trees – indifferent to
persistent pressure of the air
as damp as steam. Light cloys
translucent amber beads that
dangle from uncluttered weeds as
sinuous as living breasts that quietly
swell from tenuous ground
no tiredness left: so awkward
under banks of cloud that threaten
rain the way is shown to
wards a London where the sun
is rising & we meet again.

4

Wormed & rusty like a quarried fox
her memory dreams of tower window stars

                          Such brutes!   apparelled

in a brilliant seething rush of nothing to hear.
So she fidgets,
concealed in the name of her veil
with her gunbarrel hair
& bunches of stubby fingers in the frost

Mugs of black widow!   is the
cry as I go into her, but lost
though feeling her cream: it's cold & hard
on little purple hearts. But that was years ago
& now through window-bars   "The blue night sky
her basement memory dreams

5

Receding to views from the western boudoir
friends & old women refrain to step out in the slight
acridity. Later, these hags are poised precariously,
conscious & pleased! – ohh earthbound planets
glare on kerbside still rosettes!
Police-cape rainy streets are soaking all tonight
whether they creep alone or sleeping together

under the steam & pressure of
monstrous artificial skies –
vituperated, loathed, & longing to blaze away
at flickering eyes between the slats

That cold commemorative tale the unforgetful past
is thrashing about in a pail of our freshly drawn fears.

6

The elms' gigantic limbs, mild soft cheese
& pickles in the rain. The slight facts of the case
were terribly venomous to him,
shining through barer branches
like the sky as the season changes
like that soft starry "you"
& the tawny sky receding westward
where the stars will soon appear

in distant space that stretches deeply out
beyond our grasp, sinuous
as riverweed in the rain, as her hair
in the swollen current, oh madam we
receive but what we give
"weak, slothful, a voracious reader"

7

Whatever "this vague outline of it all . . .
afloat on the watery air, a clutter of
little zoomy puffs
                    That old song of crickets
dissolving into fields
her burning vacuous brow,
such pallid events
I'm unable to read any more

owing to optical difficulties –
the palimpsest kind,
quite often met on station platforms
so late at night & crying
                    on account of the northerly air

The lovely face of Edith Scob

7a

She had this
　　　　dimness

falling all day long, like the
quiet distance of hills

& a fiery arc of
coruscating hair
　　　　　　made up a
frail screen for her
vast green stare

& the stars will soon appear in this poem
like a politic image

like little hopeless words

like sinuous river-hair &

endless drifting
evening sky

coda

A recurring condition of the frenzied
                              is fatigue
                    & I lurch a bit
                    passing out of a Purcell
                    concert.
                              That torrid elegance
                    is abandoned as I
              pass into a week of
                    prize-winning beer which is also
        a week of concurrence in
                    self-abnegation, dappled
              with tiny shadows
                                        cast by
                    unrepresentative events
                    I'm unable to read anymore. What?
Quelle furie! – What drizzly days before the season
opens up on us, new & original as a diary
        under the rusty nibs &
              blackened blades: ". . . a
        sinister appearance in doorways, an arc of
              fiery hair, sa robe de soie
                    un brillant rouge
                                        turning/

        to the tune of 'Pannonica'

In the Grass

freezing & white again today, personally
I'm undefeated by it all, that emblematic
conspiracy, known as tea by the fire.
I don't even care if this turns into something other
than where I'd care to go, turning in & up
the steps from Millbank, don't you think the river
didn't look so cold that day, so mild for January,
didn't you think, as we took our condition in with us,
having driven down there with it, hammering under
the Blackwall tunnel on four cylinders & a car full of
mud & bits of hay

      "that's one way of eluding the sentence
  after all
    one idea is as good
 as another such as "order stinks
  & is to be
    ordered about

When one is given an idea one is stuck with it

& I'm stuck with 1

like leaving Rotterdam in 1925
or try as an alternative
    coming back in chunks
   to the Stedelijk Museum

& after all, it must be fucking nice to be
   Joseph & Mildred Gosman

Anyway kids, you know I'm no art lover
& to hell with the West

I've had several invitations
from long-legged girls, & I can accept them

as occasion permits

Maybe next weekend I'll stroll around St. Martin's
                    (Memo: must write to Barry
                                        (Flanagan)

But it's so difficult to finish anything
or else one goes unnoticed & is subsequently
destroyed.
                    It all comes down to these specific
pictorial problems
& that's my problem today, how to distract
attention from my frozen feet,

surrounded as I was by women, the
    Women, or
The Visit
            & oh my God, we're home again
        at Kettle's Yard, coming back
to that all embracing delight he had experienced
in nature stones & flowers & probably grass

            & I mean
                    GRASS!
            which I hate

& the effeminate refinements
of linear delight that's drawn into it, so much to read
into the painting, so much
Christian & Celtic mythology, contained
unmoving squares of colour without backs,
mulling themselves over in the light so
clearly imported from the other end
of the island, like the pebbles, so painstakingly
arranged

& even Gaudier
                    somehow filmic there

rotating in the light

                                       puh –

    chess   –   ka!

but colder here

                      that

fragmenting bubble

                             of softly voiced

      appreciation

                    falling

like the snow on the grass outside

Letters from Sarah (1973)

1

from time to time that which is resilient in me
retreats to more jaundiced hideaways
or I hang from a hollow tree
waiting to be cut down by a travelling lawman
who later turns out to be a bounty-hunter
or a soldier from the muddy lowlands
draws back the curtains of the bed
as somebody turns on the fountain

my little girl is standing out there in the courtyard
the hotel wardrobe as empty as my head

tell me slowly now
the shoals tremble & break up at low tide
when do you want to leave
your passport your intentions
the bridge has been destroyed by dynamite
the screws are on their way

the heavy black painting in the corner
which piece to move which lamp to choose for your pleasure
this autumn of burnt documents

I love you your quiet features in the glass
we're leaving little one
it's calmer on the island now

we display ourselves like an order of archangels
under a fusilade of white bullets

2

at the frontier we gave 'em a lot of madam
before accelerating away
to an accompaniment of whistle-blasts
into the forest a breather under the beeches
our hands & faces black with ink
the roe-deer were eating nuts or something

I got your letter & in reply to your question
I can only say that I know he already loves you etc

at the dockyard we pick up a lot of cheap bananas
there are hoists for the animals
the sails bulge as we walk by
our new secretary is a simple creature & is going out
with a right collection of villains free of charge

but this living to repeatedly break off
can one speak of the soul as a sort of inward draught?

the sky turns a brilliant yellow in the late afternoon
a devilish irritation breaks out between the fingers

I've only myself to blame for this syntactical vocation
balancing, one finger on a bottle

3

how have you lived there
without a goat
some hens

in the sunny courtyard
the king dreams away his exile
standing by the well
or walks in the vegetable garden
throwing pebbles at the
grasshoppers

the sun goes down pulling with it the last of the open sky

put the flowers in a proper vase
& place them near your bed

4

an incredibly gymnastic sniff
can give me a thrill
as does the jutting forth of your arrogant breasts
& all my years lead up to this like twists of straw
I hope to have that waltz with you when I return
& watch our bitterly clear reflections
whirling in the mirrors of the hall
o listen my love that morning in the hills of the interior
I was a deity of no importance
or a humming-bird
or a chimney-sweep
or a servant girl in pain
my mistakes are clear to me as are the crossings-out
in a very long letter
one receives in hospital
you comb your hair so conscientiously
& when I dash into the chasm for my medicine
pursued by an hysterical pack of stylists
you become as insignificant as a false passport

5

the afternoon streets were all velocity & rage of steel
but in the steadiness of seven o'clock
steam is rising soothingly
around the glass of this continual departure
which brings down fatigue in a vertical arc
& wraps the heart in an old newspaper

so the song is colder now
& I'm wearing the resonance of black
& silken embellishments to lay against the skin

how very great it would be to see you again
with shining limbs spread out like scissors
carving up memory into garden shapes
but the whistle blows   :   partons

always the same direction
the distance always expanding

6

I light a cigarette & watch the ducks in the park
the keeper's calling in the boats
reluctantly the evening lights come blinking on

on the other balcony
someone looks away
the hotel violinist starts to play

they're lighting the candles in the dining-room
the flames spread out
like a fleet in formation.

The ferns are seeding the plains of my destiny
snowing under certain pieces of reckless foolishness

7

the way you put out your fingers wavering like your eyes
this warm restraint
if you were here where my hand slides under the cover
the shops are closing
the little girls are going home along the street
soon they'll be absorbed into the shiny sides of buses

under this resonant ceiling
I wish you a cooler breeze
like a sleepless vault
or a cleansing
& the quick leap of vowels
I repeat:
the gale under the trees   the little church   those looks
of yours
which measure the depths of something

but come let's avoid the particular by invention
a seasonal appeal to your frailty & arms

there are shafts under the mountains
& my lungs are wakeful as a trainload of Tottenham supporters
midgets for beer & madness

8

the fever & obscurity of our organisms
the matchless flowers of

in the snow of the interior

only touch me
& I'm brittle as a snail-shell
at the edge of this broad white country
all colourless wind & poplars

who gives a damn anyway
drooly girls with blue umbrellas
are bombing along the slide

drops of ink the flowery envelope

9

so lay yourself closer to the earth
& learn the secrets of iron & wine
this shapeless land will never coalesce
though wads of snow fatten the mountains
the dark roads soften to cheese

& in the spaces between the peaks
thin rays of light will turn
like the spokes of a bicycle wheel

10

(i)

teeth like yellow gravel
dance on the stem of your pipe

(ii)

some oppressively physical sounds
from room 27

(iii)

pipe composure

(iv)

why don't we take the road for Cologne?

(v)

in my brainpan
some abbreviated ideas
like button mushrooms

11

Benjamin leaves his chair & walks up the hill
moving neither his idea of himself
nor the hill
nor the shackled man
nor the old tram-lines
sunk in the tarmac
understanding only the line of parked cars
he means nothing other than himself
a pair of legs walking on marble
throws away in the street
what he no longer needs

does he put out his language
or is he soothed by a star
as he tears out his tongue
in the last part of winter?

the hemisphere tilts
the second version of the year begins
as hair & nails turn down

as the stars
zip by last night

I learn something new about you
paper friend

making a call in
the wings

you fly away to where there are
streams to adore

& sheep aspire
to your royal favour

13

"pass the salt & then the wine

the diesels howl in the night
while we in secret dine . . ."

the candles flare up in the draught

he was quite dead, his face
firmly planted in the pine needles

wearing the same old overcoat

illuminated by torchlight
the pale flight of an owl
decorated the ceiling

the adverse wind
rattling the weathercocks

the bandage yellowing on my arm

14

hey lanky one
in your double mask
come near me of your own accord
with tired limbs
your opinions of no special importance
& ambiguous blue blood

when you stand in front of my head
cool your gratuitous desire

trail yourself over this couch for a while
& enjoy the tainted light
which floats up from the harbour

later we'll set out again

15

don't turn your head & colour when you
glance my way your smile
as though you ate the sun for breakfast

sleep when you're tired put me away
between the two long lines that hold you tight
the cable cars the heights
you'll want to fish those glacier streams

there's an old char
smelling as clean as a chemist's shop
a white-painted house
& cereals
spooky flutes
that play at night

stay horizontal
if you wish to go there

16

we will go, clouds
to the Falkland Isles
arriving like Skotch Mist
over the crepuscules
we'll shade the hills a darker green

Goodbye little dress-shop boys & girls,
an affirmation passes with us
like a morning frost in June

leaving the oak-trees to their doom
an almanac in each of them

Striking the Pavilion of Zero (1975)

      for the snow
to melt into the earth of mountains

watching for dawn
in an oppressive bedroom
all that water piped away & into fountains
in the municipal squares

wanting the dawn
though a wavering moment in the dark
may hold something at least
that may last, though you can't always see

what it is you appear to want.   Well,

oblivion finally is extended
whether in the occasional insouciance of sleep
or to the sacredly drunken it settles
over the dusty pavements

                  & then the little birds fall upwards
                  & across the sky
                  from chimney to chimney

& among the folds
of clean white table linen
the glasses are poured & waiting redly

                  so das strömende Wort
                      the onrushing
              may still be granted & holy
                  remembrance also
                nothing'll be forgotten
              either tomorrow
                          or by night

Talking in Bed

1

Always it seems, the burbling trumpets
　　　wave you goodbye you wave me
　　　goodbye slow dawns before the film
　　　　dispatches the rolling wheels of cars
　　　encouraged by harpsichords
Gently the rise is breasted
　　　you found the river the
　John Burns in dry dock for repairs
　an island with trees
　no traffic wardens where you were. ". . . Only
　24 hrs . . . & the spider brushed against
　your lovely adam's apple
　as it descends over your sleeping
　through Willis Conover & again
　in 1968 I'm left alone in sneezes
　under the dusty beeches Martin
　glimpsed through Collett's window
　steaming in his impossible green rain-cape. Impossible
　things French in English poems
　are so, well, stale, like an old *Paris Review*
　as it flops from your fingers goodnight

2

Watch out for further exfoliations in
our casual blasé mean & cocky
how-would-you-like-a-punch-in-the-nose
attitude. It comes naturally to us,
what with our history of navigation and our
national service in the Polish cavalry.
            I stole that hyphenated line
                          from the work of
        a 27-year-old poet from Tulsa
        who recently "spent" a year in Paris.
From an article entitled 'But I only wanna get started right away'
& what with Martin shortly transferring his attentions
to La Joie de Lire
& with all this plagiarism
we are reverted naturally to France –
on a cheap day excursion from Folkestone, of course.
After all, things Deutsch in English poems
are so, hem, well, faded & abstract,
like a Tauchnitz edition of *Tarr*
as it finally flops
& steams in the clouds at the base of your spine

pointless
                    the boatman praising
                      the breeze in the calm
                   bland & relaxed
                      the obdurate telephone
             cables ease through woolly leaves
             too much rumpled paper in the basket
             & after dinner, a third pint taken more sedately

                   "to leave Goethe out of it
                                    Ted, is that too
                   harsh? But it's so difficult
                      & even seductive.
                             These islanders
                         imagine English as formidable –
                   as if Greenwich really were
                      the centre of the universe

                       "I rue the day" he sighed. "You feel
             anything at all? These pinnacles
                   are so theatrical & it
                      snowed so in Goslar

                 But, astonishing & unconcerned,
             darkness approaches the treetops,
                   miserable & lurid

                      o fucking privet bleeding
                      Vögelein, belt up!
                   we feel quite alien to your swarthy
                                      droppings

uuhhh?

hacchh!

      his abrogated situation
                     the rain
   not my friend's, not any one of them
was it a trifle recidivist of me
                to choose
    Ornette? this morning
              has all the insistence
   of reiterated financial
           difficulties
        & is hence
    PRIVATE & CONFIDENTIAL, by
virtue of its separation
          from unthatched
       events
   back in the distant market

in fact
    the usual problems
even without a post
         & my favourite trousers
   left at Sketchley's again, the only clean
   those passé naval whites
    bought out of desperation
 somewhere on the
         Portobello

Good God! Is this the bathroom or the sepulchre?
     real sabbath trousers
      indeed (my address to the curly fungus

vorwärts!   you fan heaters

meanwhile there's always my Brut
to fall back on. Or,
I speak to the leaves
but they can't listen to me

how unecstatic of them

                    a complete innocence
          may be given us on completion
          like an irrelevant myth
which floats out into language
          with a light caressing
          urgency, or I may recall
               the inviolate, no more disturbing than
          the distracting chatter of the little
               sparrows, how French you seem
                    now as a recollection
          your face strung out along the beanpoles
          a faint wish turning the entire world
               into an erotic object:
          you are the current name
               of a most impossible condition

     so near, the cruel uncertainties of love

Rough

for Rolf Dieter Brinkmann

if you don't know German
flicking over the pages of *Die Piloten*
again the poems I'd like to translate

so many lovely words   :   Luft   Tod
Büstenhalter   I'd like a pint   it's hot
the clouds are glum

but it's after closing-time
& I haven't a thought in my head that could
sound like a line of Hölderlin

fishing the Old West River
the wind blew hard in my face all day
it does that any time it likes, forever

but it's quieter here in the attic
I don't need to be amused
I can make my own coffee as strong as I like

best to die in summer
when everything is bright
& the earth turns over lightly

the day writhes in an immense crater
some gleams want to burst out now & then
but further off on the taut horizon
the wind moves hardly at all it becomes
necessary to wait for the voices to return I
put down the pen get up & fasten all the doors

& soon the painted gauze descends once more
it looks like you again but with the centrepiece mislaid
the parti-walls tilt back revealing the greater sky
where a star comes loose & a shadow runs over
everything closes up on itself a
single occasion in the time continually piling up
but when will I be able to come to the moment
when it's possible to finish everything & begin again
you never look at me when will you be able to come back

it's only a game but oh so steadfast we keep on
passing the brink of an elegant nothing though
sometimes something in us makes everything tremble
& then the world doesn't exist anymore
or else we're mistaken & it merely makes a different sound

then it's yourself you see behind the universe
a dancing silhouette in a series of portraits
you fail to recognise any of them
but they're family you're looking at
in the middle of those motionless faces
the only one who's living is apparently the most placid
he leaves never to return

in the room where the walls are beginning to smile
it's only the night which gets up to leave
it's getting cold
your attention rises toward the stars

drawing my chair closer to the speaker
I'm carried by a level wave
or the ghostly hobby-horse of my senseless youth
everything was on show there
in that innocent world of chinking silver pennies
though nobody bothers here either
& I drag my cable
taut with all that pulls me back
though I'd rather not mention what we already know
we fooled around in the Gorsedd Gardens
& now it's failed us entirely
we throw out all the implements & run away
trailing our shadows over the Cotswolds
the field succumbs to a single blow of the hook
& the fierce heat of our electric blankets
ashen I look for the pass & it's cold
but the day gets up & lights a fire
& the dusk contracts to the room where I'm sitting
everything's closed up like the world & my soul was too
before it jumped out of a little hole in my knee
& I caught a glimpse of your back
as it leapt over the wall
each stone keyed to the other

27 October 1969

for Barry Flanagan

There are some lights & we will name them, thus:-

    1, the flax & the wood

    2, the wood

  & the flaxen arrow of

        your hair is shorter this afternoon
        a pale grey light at the back of your head

        & recently snipped
        a few tiny hairs

        little creases in the arms of your jacket

& in the top of the flax

          the one suspended
          curving fold

  a neat dark shirt
  no fuss

  perspicuous gaze
  walking out on a rainy pavement in Bern

  "hmmmm"

the rope demolishes its own presence

the rods

the tilting perspective of the wall
the white slightly scuffed where it joins the floor

the ominous corner

the panache of flax in air

polish

3 long sticks

Will the points?

right, not even paint

to a depth of three inches

The Dragon House

her bright green leather high-heeled pumps

draws back the curtains to the sun & coffee in bed
on trays with legs this windscreen of a morning
moving with beech & yew a stewpond full of goldfish

I would wish to attend to nothing more than that
which is the measure of a lack of prayer

how could I be able to propose anything other?

the way the ice melts all along your back
that soft declivity near your tail

the sun warms through the glass
we drank last night
little yellow cups of Prunelle Noyer & now
what litters today?
a pile of pastoral trousers & an old straw hat
a pale blue notebook bought in Hannover . . .

discard *The White Stones*
open on the quilt at p.71
finish the coffee
& sniff the smoky November day

which is thrashing about in the poplars
& looking more like poplars in the wind today
though otherwise the life of plants is not so

powerfully bedraggled here, the garden
ordered as a circulating library
soft romance & too much glare
for my watery eyes.
                              So here we all are
                              & here we all are then
                              like a hardy 70-year-old
                              stripped to the waist
                              all tan & grizzled
                              in the gale
& here is the day with its clouds, a Sunday,
& we're writing & reading & checking our oven controls
& wondering if after lunch to become spectators of the
        unbeatable
base-line-school-of-old, just-get-it
over-the-net-child-or-you'll-spoil-the-game
Diana versus the locals &
Smarden   Bethersden   Appledore
foreign as white clapboard houses
windmills   a curious zeitgeist never very far away
the clouds are getting up from the west
I think it's going to pour with rain, lunch
can't be very far away either as you have this pain
you think is hunger so you eat, you eat too much
& so you are "in pain again"

                              yellow tomatoes
I particularly like
                    what is
Wendy doing in the orchard? She has cut
either a cauliflower
or a . . . "your English vegetables are so good, all you need
is to prepare them in an American way . . . " so I duck
out under the eaves again, hunting for postcards

& send one with love to:

> Master B. MacSweeney,
> 90b The High Street,
> Barnet,
> Herts.

Now it's the turn of
the shrivelled roses. Luckily
she doesn't have her towalong basket, her gumboots
riding mac & floppy flowered summer hat the brim
held down & tied at the chin with a chiffon scarf
of blue or green, ahhh, quick, shut the curtains!
this continuous sun! O rum
bustuous machine, redolent of Picabia,
his *Parade Amoureuse*, rattle
the rafters, the wall & quietude of Grandmama
Daubeney Russell-Clarke her grey eternal smile
enthralls me working freely in the morning though the
easing of the light is also good before Britannia
pulls down her shades of a wintry evening, yes
the piano please Diana, *F minor Prelude* pushing it away
like pressing buttons
or small clear bells
that sphere out lighter from themselves
against the indolence of the loggy room

What to those fabulous flying creatures carved & white?

Good Old Harry

we go to sleep like anybody else
though some awake like bullets
like Romans
munch munch

we aren't Romans
we aren't Americans either
we drink a lot of beer
every nation has its own greatness

we are the English
easy-going & lazy
we sleep pretty well
& when we wake

we are usually pretty thirsty
but not for anything too drastic
you can trust us to be
wooden & quietly proud

of our laver bread
our dumplings
a tomato or two
does no one any harm

& if there did happen to be a bullet amongst us
it would never find anywhere to go
it would just keep travelling through the air
without hitting anything

we have thirty-eight rulers
which is very economical
& they are well protected from
tomatoes on the whole

we call them the cabinet
& cupboard is the name of the land
where everything is in its place again
the natural rulers

behaving like proper gentlemen again
eating a bit of cabbage
& sausage now & then
like the rest of us no doubt

when Edward goes for a walk
we take off our caps & wave them in the air
England is a mature nation
& is not a bit like America

The Grace

1

back where the old fantastical night & the snow
ingested by dawn & the earth of mountains
far from the city which is never dark
that other darkness
turbulently piped away

will it be when lost in brutal places
or where in municipal squares
the shadowy white plumes rise to him
at the moment of a kerbside hesitation
when he returns he remembers her face
under the stern mounds of speechless tenements & spires

there

2

her private history of alms
clubs lending libraries

her sundry weaknesses
perhaps she's a little in their power

& afraid of beginning
till her benevolent mood returns

because if she does she may be
cold perfunctory official

should they take liberties
as she fancies

she can give them a pill
or she might go out again

till her benevolent mood returns
& she lays down for him

a thing to be improved
whatever else I say

the trees are pliant to the wind
a glider takes advantage of

a seasonal delay
however close a way

where berries & this love of her
do sometime grow a

shiftless craving to be under camouflage
will never do : as the bows

of a laden freighter quietly enter
that patch of blue which is the sea

I'll be at the kerbside
a walker to order like a green alarum

so there's an end both to lamentation &
the harsh cries of the newsvendor

I tune in to another programme
pressing & clicking my molars

from the earth quite gratefully transmuted
as the hammer rings upon my breast
starblin & blest

an interior happy change is made
& you become less bald
unswapped unstamped & meliorate

by such means the suffering land
find grace & mastery
to cure debauchery

Going Back to Sleep 2:12 p.m.

The sheets are white
the four walls of my heart are grey
as the sky is grey
                      & the air
in my head over you
goes on singing over the blue carpet
                      everywhere
so blue & so grey
                      here in the Saxon heartland

a dangerous wind & temptress to exalted nihilism
as we continue with prodigious cheerfulness & speed
breaking off to this unforeseen departure from agreements
to celebrate a peaceful crescent moon
our quiet freedoms

I am surrounded by men & women whose music pleases me
            in the evening
            walking in the park
                        or at my fireside
transgressing the limits of their sterility
with opium, whisky, the dance, talking
                        or simply listening with grace

            more & more acute
            & thin the air

            climbing out on top of our heavier satisfactions

                the frailer women there
            but desperately more beautiful & more oblivious
            the men with a reflexive calm
            consider their next moves

        Years of spirit genius engineering
            & of northern sun

Proleptic

some casuist palming a sixpence
or thoughts of the heart of man
which is not as beautiful as a football stadium
or is as beautiful as a football stadium
home of the married people
you ask how old the captain is
the light in the clouds
bathing the odeon
gives nothing away
the pavements in my part of town are purple & grey
I recline at ease in my armchair
an orgy of barbarism obliges me to write something today
galloping through the neck
inconsequential as water
or *Peter Getting out of Nick's Pool*
I shall give myself up to art
the preoccupation of dull & stupid women
supine art & supremely useless poetry
which makes me ache with laughter
as quick as a name caught on the breeze
when the sun looks as if it's going to disappear behind some
    clouds
I pick up my cup again & go back down to the kitchen

May Day Greetings 1971

eating a plate
from day to day
sharper than ever

blow your nose
in authentic
rigorousness

advance to bonheur

A Theory of Poetry (1977)

it's very important
to make your lines
bands of alternating colour
running from one side to the other

these will bind
your poem together
like an egg
& make it exist

a reticulated broken edge
the positive ingredients of
banality & repetitiveness preferable
to histrionic virtuosity on most occasions

indeed be dogged
it's better to be expressively dumb
than full of mediocre elegance
& bullshit

& though expensive paper will provide
the physicality your poem needs
you can also apply a bit of boot polish
to transparently tinted over-painting

& in this act of obliteration
performed in a fusion of
calculation cynicism & fervour
the poem will suddenly realize itself

this will subvert any/ deny any/ positive/negative
narrative reading
& stress the written surface
with all its openings windows apertures leaks

& the incongruity of this literalness & frivolity
will induce in the reader a greater objective awareness

reading is often a big help
but wherever you turn
you are surrounded by language
like the air

you will find the difficulty of working this way
makes you long to be

another kind of poet
however try to be stringent & lean
as well as luscious from time to time

assert the bodily means
by which your poem is written
after all
as the man said
thought
is in de mouf

standing out
luxuriant & mundane
against the subtlety of English light
which is the foil

you can afford to be less cerebral
less intellectual less brilliant less clever
less locked-up-in-your-room-at-night-ish
less reticent & deferential

& more programmed flatter
more all-over more environmental
always
on the prowl

for the materials
of your existence
in the city
which is sometimes what is meant by spirit

get as much as possible into
sitting-rooms bathrooms bedrooms
kitchens & hotels
gardens parks & streets & saloon bars

there you will discover
particular people at a particular time
& in a particular place
these people are the others
without whom you would not exist

avoid the countryside unless
you are going to do something there
like ascend Helvellyn
or shoot a brace of partridge to take back to your kitchen

useful activities include
eating talking & dancing
listening to music (preferably live bands
looking at paintings & undressing
dressing & undressing

do not be too overawed
by wide open spaces
love France by all means
but love your own language first

that way it will be of your own
as well as your own
& will be trusted by neighbours
& summer visitors alike

& thereby your formal relations
untempered by such vulgar considerations as taste
can adjoin
crude broken ridges

overlaid by sluggishly dragged bands of the drab & blaring
can adjoin
delicate smears & caresses
that

War (1978)

If you/you feel like/you ave no reason for
living/gosh/don't determine my life/my life
DOCTOR ALIMONTADO

Is she really/
& she sd bring him near me
one step nearer
& I'll deck him
big as she is
the fat cow
she'll stab your back
like a dream in Permanent Black
what was the/what was the masked fireman
coping/
the fire in the freezer chest
will she ever/
the language of your mortal peers
crawls from your lips
pronouncing
the word kind
but doing a kindness
is not therefore kind

What's your name anyway?

Veronica/Veronica what/
Veronica what's-the-difference
inscription is its own form of condescension

but there are certain things in life
which have the power to restore you to your senses
such as chorizo sausage
& the works of James Osterberg
strike at the bone
at the back of the ear
like a bowl of exploding radish

Cruising

hard behind the next a foul smelling
perfume of decaying brilliance like a
diamond thinly coated in excrement

Friday in my mind again
saliva in my eyes
days of no past
let alone 'no future'
so he goes
I seem to remember
being egged by Sunday
what happened to Saturday?
gone like any other day of wire
a typical Monday
a typical Tuesday
welcome to the working week
but I've got Friday on my mind again &
days of loaded zippers
days of falling in love with X & Y
days of shaving my legs again
never wanting to

squelching under trucks
on the waste
it certainly is
no fun

secedes to a cold hush
& scars it madly
every morning the sun rises
but not everywhere
hello fine winter
it's a very good November again
October was very good also, so was
autumn summer & last winter was
pretty good too
although I can't remember much about it

zinc

seated at the bar
I gave him one of my
nothing-doing looks &
smiled over his left shoulder
where you were adjusting
an eyelash

(Feminist studies pimp in interesting denim
creature of an easy recognition)

Sid never picked up
on things like that, but after an encounter
someone else would have to tell him/
You really frightened that person
but it/
but it's being who you are
& doing what you want to do
& being left alone to do it

(John sd)

it takes a woman like her to get through to the man in you

we just do it

our past three years of earnest daily thoughts
shadows deeds cares & pleasures
& after all I haven't even had to eat
my own legs yet
& sexual reasons make a difference
as do tyranny & deceit
& flapping your tie in my face/
oh, a *nice* set of buttocks

& all else flesh/
lilac but neutral
under its bruises

I wouldn't entertain it

if you wish to avoid hanging – tell 'em nothing!

& a creepy species of invert
ed sexism
could just outlast our days

&
till
the
mouth
opens
we don't
know what
s going
to come
out

talk to me as I sit on the sofa in the corner, but I
won't answer . . .

kind is a world/is a word
lacking intention
like a chip done in Frymax

our usual friendly pub
with its sinister air of normality it say
"The work is done, the die
is cast/
another sodding day is past

enough, you're such a liar

| enough. For the Rich Kids The Future Is Financial.

they (whoever they
may be
  shoot the shot
  that echo
  round the world first
& ask questions afterwards he
(Robert Creeley) say/they
     we know

LONDON 1977 BORED PRESSURE HATE & WAR

  48 HRS DENY CAPITAL

POLICE CHEAT   REMOTE CAREER

  JANIE RIOT

I must have fallen into a thornbush
or the typical anonymity of Lowestoft
which we like
falls around your shoulders
like a cold shower of eels

SPLOSH
KISH

till finally
terrorised by the birds
& blinded by the nasty yellow flowers
back at the hotel
we relax with a copy of *Country Life*

do you feel it when you look at the fire?

listen kid, when you're in love with a married woman
you shouldn't wear mascara

there I was/
eating my breakfast in my honeysuckle arbour
reading the Irish American poets
in the pure sphere of nothing to achieve
when a shout carries over from the end of the street/
SOLES ALIVE
SOLES ALIVE

& I get the distinct impression of the
opaque presence of an old Nazi

I got your letter & in reply to your question
I can only say I don't know
there's a flashing blue light
but there's also a strong smell of burning onions

(Exhibition at Checkpoint Charlie)

don't knock fresh bread if you've always had plenty
on the shelf

By the year 2000
blood will be approaching fingertips

then there was this terrible outburst
of over meticulous inventiveness
& if I close my eyes
it will not go away
just a little grey lint to read you by

                                    TOM + ALV

           WARNING!
        NO-GO AREA FOR NF PIGS!
THE WORLD FOR THE PEOPLE OF THE WORLD
                              YEAH

           GASELEE STREET
                E14

you'd better believe it we mean it man we
don't know nothing to do with another world
either down or up
I & I are still living in the same world
since I am born

if you can leave yourself alone to write it

short
stay

long
stay

subway

i confront my elbow
begging to be normal

the 80s
start here ⟶

2,000 detainees

a very monotonous sound/
propping you/head against the wall

stripped to the neck
where the black hood starts
shaking a warning out of the ooze of Essex skies

DO YOU WANT TO BE PART OF THE FUSCHIA?
GET OUT OF THAT GARDEN!

One of the half dozen soldiers
involved then asked the driver
to go slowly. In the next few
minutes
16 times
the cuts
require

so we screw the quarterlies
on the newspaper test/

The white dots are members of the crowd
The black dot is you.
You desperately need to get to the bar.
Can *you* find the way?

going up the pike with only a teaspoon
& a can of Corimist

(cough)

a rissole or two
does no one any harm
sulphate & beer are also
very good indeed

& prime the music
of the land
a green illuminated text
in vintage telecaster headlamp blur
just outside the drawn yellow curtains

ohh garrulous earthlings
speeding like a sabotage of hares
watch out for further exfoliations in
our casual blasé mean & cocky
how-would-you-like-a-punch-in-the-nose
attitude

wear it short but loose
& full off your head
but strip your neck to the nape
not for my sake
but as a gift

A Former Boiling (1979)

A Former Boiling

for The Human League

if you're going to do it then do it OK/Good Day
Good Day/this is Radio Shack

calling/or if that's Radio Ethiopia
this is Radio Splott/calling

home the Nation/
voice of Philip Oakley in a huge tincan

tasty dribbles on the side of a mentor
like the spillings on a can of beans

blast from the Frigidaire
like a draught on the outcome
a shiver leading to a xerox on the Underground/

but if this is sericulture
that was torture in a million little ways
a synthesiser whiplash that I couldn't hear

entailing star flange damage
or do I mean star point damage/

under the fire of prolix tongues
I do hear Voices/in the H-BLOCKS calling/
saying DESTROY/saying

        call her mother fourthly blest
        noble lady to our race

        just because you call her mother
        doesn't mean that she's a nutter

she the queen who decks her subjects
on a kind of hairy vest

mother's calling mother's waiting
but the towel's splashed with shit

mother's waiting mother's calling
splice the children in a line/

splice the children on a rope
then wonder why we all take dope/

~

O COUSIN PAT OF BLEEDING CELT FLESH
remember the unforgettable torture of the Fifties
blipping out of a hole in
the razored insanity of the Fifties when Mutual Assured
Destruction was the only deterrent
between siblings & Nation States
your sons & daughters won't forget/the
curtain blue TV light/freezing on the streets/that
they're-in-there & you're-out-here feeling

from which we get the word inherent
or a lime-twig on the tree-line
which later gave way to the Hotline
in the dream of that Almost All Over In Habana Line
yes that was still the Fifties Too line
later becoming the snow-line
on the Picadilly Line
which was later to become the Dicanol Line
& Tales of Other Stigmata Line/

THIS AIN'T NOSTALGIA/THIS IS EXORCISM/This is

Demonology/Martyrology
Pressure-ology/
            biology

on strictly spiral time

the hair combed in a quiff line

On the Dubinski line
on the Strinati line
on the O'Mahoney O'Connor O'Leary line
on the Theresa line
the Maria line
the Clare & Bernadette line
on the Somebody's Digging Your Potatoes line
on the potatoes npoint line
on the Fresh-bread-can-taste-so-good line
on the Fasting since Midnight line
or the Thou who art called the Paraclete
Send us something down to Eat line

on the No Exceptions line
the take no prisoners line
the give no quarter line
on the Crimson Host in the Tantum Ergo line
on the Burning Bread in the Therefore How Much My Lord line
on the trains coupling in the night in the sidings
on the Republican Clubs line

on the What Are We Doing Here line
on the Babylon line
on the tell 'em nothing line
on the Origin of the British Army line
on the suppression of the Irish people & the defence of the
        Protestant religion line
the Cold War miscarried out of that line
on the years ago in Germany line
on the why don't nobody mention it line

on the Alexander Pope line
on the road from Trenchtown line
on the road from Newtown line
on the I & I line
on the Kevin Barry line
on the Tom Barry line
on the Michael Collins line
on the Who Shot Michael Collins line
on the how many boys in your school were called Michael
    Collins line
on the Lord Boyd of Merton line
the they're-at-it-again line
on the Alan Lennox-Boyd line

HO   LA

HO   LA

which is the Back To Africa line
on the Silurian line
the ultimate reunification of Ireland
on the Rock Island Line
our island in the future line
he lifts up the stones on Inishmore

on the give me some more of those potatoes line
at the Convent of the Sisters of Providence line
on the Come Holy Ghost Creator come line
you used to see her on the number 12 bus line
on the Portmanmoor Road line
on the Shirley Bassey's Drunk Again on the
Was There Ever Poetry In The Fifties line
on the Hound Dog line
on the Heartbreak Hotel

on the Sitting on the Botany Bay line

on the yes-father no-father line
on the rhythm method line
but the withdrawal line
is an Excommunication line
an if-you-vote-Labour-you-do-so-under-peril-of-mortal-sin line/

~

BUT THE STARS BURN ABOVE & BELOW HER HEAD ON
    HABERSHON STREET
As Pat Kisses The Blistering Cheek Of The Acolyte
under the enamel pelican that tears its own breast
black pudding again for tea
tears & dripping & milky balm
the hard-on against your soft brown pleated skirt
in the alley your shaking fingers over the purple head line
on the spurting arc line
the little cries of ah line
on the middle finger line
the scars of dried semen on your brown stocking line
they caned us on the hand line

~

Screw-up/Close-up
closure on the East Moors/the line of steel on the dole queue

& Uncle P got £x,000 compo to reinvest in Ladbroke's
after the rain of ash on Marion Street
still killing Patsy's mother after all those years
on the Woodbine line/the Meggazone line
the That'll make an interesting footnote line
on the box & cox for furniture line
on the cardboard box for cots line
on the we-never-want-to-go-back-to-those-days-again line
on the Tories Are Vermin/Shock Horror Headline
the hook-worm line/
the Carrington is an unelected parasite on the Nation

no secret ballot for him/the
Hook in the RTZ line
but Jim loved Julian more than Splott
& who made Ernest Bevin's line
or the Old Thunderer's First Leader line
the that line is up line
the 38th parallel running like a dotted line
through the onset of Patsy's puberty
a clotted line of blood on the pavement of Sanquhar Street
on The Who said we won't get fooled again line

on The Severn Tunnel as Borderline
on the GWR & So Away To
Sing Out All You Miners line
on the Taff Vale Iine
the Annie Powell line
on the Pen-y-graig line
on the Ystrad Rhondda line
on the green star liner/the black star liner
on the Red Star Train Soon Come

⁓

& on the Bromley Contingent Line
the Don't Forget Your Jumper line/
thrown out of Twilight Sleep
under that blaring sky
leaping out of their Pans in the Heat of the Suburban Night
& on the QV for the Permafrost
on the Bean Time line
on the Bean-Sidhe line
on the line-out line
on the rising line
JHP & Siouxsie-Sioux make the feathered jump to Hyper Space

Pure Chainsaw feeling in the Vat of TLP
The Enemy of TV/The Enemy of Slow Decay
the hard line on the fall-out line
The Polish Cavalry Boot on the Iron Curtain line
The Who Left This Tank In Here Piece
metal on creaking metal
on this level crossing line
the on the line line
on the bands of alternating colour
on that distant planet line
the Cousin Patsy didn't know you when she walked on Planet
    Street line
on the line of the nearest party
right down the line of a fierce fatigue
on the queue for the gods
it's a busy line
What's Your Game
What's Your Number
What's Your Line

Toasting (1979)

Look all around/ yeah
Tapper Zukie

working away in a miniature Babylon in the muddy lowlands
north of the city can be hard you know/the indications:
slow rural Tory pull in a mixed gig dimension of town
& gown aggression/heavy discipline overflank the people
under Jesus & the Redevelopment Corporation/the old
Eastern Association long ago sunk deep into the land/
1,000 slum dwellings & reveries of a quick come profit
hidden behind the sunning facade of the members room
at County Hall/no Red Stripe at the Midland either

but when the massive skies ride over
dispelling the lactic smear
you can look up there

& the presence of JULIA BALL her little studio over
in old Red Abbey on the east side of town near the
river & Stourbridge working on the light

                                        /that

whole flat range of the tenuous run of fen against the sky
green or tawny as amber in the skin the skin as damp as steam
broad shining grid of land & water
the changing light & colour collecting in a concentrated
pool on Quy

of which she has made a cache
a series/a stash of classic English water-colour
conserving her love of that place & her eye for it/
from which she works in continuous dub
echo & dub

the drift & climb of cloud at evening
the tilt & lift of earth at evening
into that slow bleed long horizon
are her almost basement memory dreams

as the season changes
over & over again the same new land
month to month & year by year until her eye
returning from Malaysia & Iran
unveiling pale grey milk delusion
goes into that part again
the pool at Quy
become the window in the mosque at Qom
the eye itself the crescent & the moon
the aperture/small curving split in the back of the hand
blue purple moving dark & soft/blue moving into green
& driving down from Liverpool in early May
unable to forget the crescent bleed contracts & splits
to mark a crusting pulse/the lengthening horizon of the august

I tell you/

Max Jacob/he say
it would be ordinary enough to live in that glittering Ethiopia
dreaming the dream that no one has the power to evict
the towels white with orange borders
boats with brown sails on dark blue seas
& buildings small enough to live in yes/
I'm talking about KIT WOOD/his black his white
red cheek & chalk/& oh that blue is it Ripolin blue/
over the heads of the *Dancing Sailors*/a
painting as if there was no tomorrow/
nothing descriptive or prescriptive/just clean paint
feeling clean outside the vacant head/yeah
              we like coffee we like tea
              we like boatsn we like sea

our laver bread/our dumplings/
boiled beef & carrot/
new coat & boat/
uncertainty & electric daylight

Paris take no heed of (limblessly in love with dreams) of
the sleeper/glistening sand/
dreaming the nightmare of the head as plastic bag
the yellowing flesh the Staffordshire dogs/
Big Youth on Cheyne Walk ageless & young
the plate is sliding out of the canvas
her plate her sliding out of her head
cousin O of blushing Celt flesh
throat smelling of clean young skin
under the devouring sniff of a nasal search
hard & bloody like the guts of thousand dogfish
painting & writing all day & meeting at meals

       but we live among the freaks in Luna Park
       with postcards for our company at night

many many rockas leaving town/a kind of civic leak
into & out of the world outside
the struggle for what is light in what is dark
shine to advantage in our backyard/

love of the creatures shine from the haunts of memory again/

catching/random lamp-post bisections/
red cars in Bournemouth &
Wolverhampton flowerbeds & walls flags &
occluded objects that may not be there
heavy discipline of fixture & fittings/
stopped clocks & the trappings of secret & minor
local rites & customs/like getting on & off buses etc

Red Stripe/grey stripe

SHORT STAY

LONG
STAY

SUBWAY

each stripe in the depot glows like a spinning florin
no waste in the fragments torn & traced in the rivers of space
left us in the imprint made by others/
all you others

'The postcard does not constitute proof that anything
happened or that anything was any colour or that there
were clouds in the sky'
                                    –TOM PHILLIPS/

or silver lustre
in a 3:00 a.m. shop window mannequin
under provincial neon light/she goes

a correspondence of approach hidden beneath a difference
of appearances/

each strip on the *Greys*
each band of alternating colour in a HODGKIN
a thought of a line/a thought of a trace of a line
a run from one side to the other of the page

or in the bedrooms
or in the kitchens with the avocados
or in the little gardens/
out to lunch & out for drinks with X & Y/all luscious
paint that's in the world & up against the subtlety
of English light/
stress on the written surface
the whole flat range of the shifting land/
the whole flat range of the shifting surface

in PETER CARTWRIGHT/graduations of tone/
plateau edge of menace under sharp constraint of line/
after the drift of endless stellar sky
homelings coming back in '67/
rockas coming back to Camden town in 1967
after the outer planet lights the dawn thing suddenly on us

[174]

axe-cut defile & Valley scarp/the surface scudding under
machine machine/the envelope opening thigh & hanging over
capsule into fuming Glenmorangie
talk in Jeremy's white panel room
in paranoid opening '70/

& now it really get down there
& open up on us/

on PHILIP CROZIER
with the big stain paintings of that year
spilling enamel & acrylic burst mountain
cobalt & vermilion park & recreation field
the melting Thames-side skies
spatter of yellows over the Mudchute

the drawings for *Sarah*
scratched in the void with elementary
school ink pen & drawing smell of mark in space
& wall & THIS WAY OUT to smoke & cloud & flame
fall round the ziggurat
our hands & faces smudged
with preliminary utterance

but the sky turns a brilliant azure in early afternoon
the splotch the loop the swirl
give way to marine breezes
the resonant ceiling of the vault is broken
& it's back to Africa

via *Savannah*

& the verve & cool excitement of *Eastern House* looks
like the work of someone in England who still enjoys
painting & is taking us
off the street & out of the flak

the cadmium light of the inner city the

very humdrum interior of the nation
from Charing Cross Road to Aston-le-Wall to Kentish Town
the steady light at the back of the head of FLANAGAN
perspicuous gazer
over rainy pavement shine/

hmmmm

where have all the painted RSJs?

panache of flax in air & wood/
& bamboo canvas sisal rope & sand
sacking & hessian
linoleum & cord
ease over into being

the rope loosens its singularity by its assertion
of the space of the room/the wobbling blue cones of
Four Casb remove their hats/

wall edges to corner to wall/ceiling to wall to floor
speak/& muslin & sand
become themselves
trailing their skirts/
the purest heap in the world

                         meanwhile

in *Collection* days/BRUCE MCLEAN as man a warrior
DMs in the air fistfallen tinhat backwards
into the pebbles on the beaches of the Thames at Barnes
doing: 'Bye bye black bird work' a sort of wave or hand piece
& 'Artists who make Art in Glass houses Piece' from
'King for a Day' + 999 other pieces/works/things etc
including 'the piece a minute show' & 'The Fastest
speed sculpture piece in the World piece' & the proposal for
a retrospective show: 'The Universal Crimble Crumble
Spectacular', 'Heh there you with the Art in your eyes!'

& the much raved about Flip Flop works/
early days of digging in for later assaults as:

Jerry Lee Lewis Killer & Iron thief of Banal Gesture as
Arousal Assassin Banger of the lover of the Deep Freeze
Murderer of Monumental Aspiration
Slayer of the Merely Mercantile & P & I
Gothic Vandal of the Over-Posed Home
Fairex the Liberator of the Chair Person from the Hedgemony
of the Anglepoise Lamp Habitat & Sainsbury Time Out Curfew
& Founder Leader of the SFPHBIA

what the time you have there Natty?/ /LONG

                                              time

a very early man/

the aboriginal walker mover/projecting & carrying his weight
crossing & recrossing rivers
projecting his line
The Garden of England reverses into the future
beaming backwards before the plough
the mark of the foot
on the page of the earth
stone & clay beneath his feet
across roads across bridges
making his way
& showing his hand
he walks the line
the tie that binds
the city to the rock
& marks the distance with his eye
& the line has an edge
of its own & a speed of its own

& a map of its own &
a line outside the self he
lifts up the stones on Inishmore
in a place on the foreshore where there are no paths
every large stone in the Primary place on the foreshore
where there are no paths to read them by
we have to read them by their own
limits outside device & sign
limits of the physical strength involved
without artifice or motive other than the compulsion
to go down there & wrestle in the Rock in
desolate places
wilderness where I & I are in this place
beyond the sound
under the harmless skies
precedent of the plough & metaphysic

a man was here/a line in the Himalayas
carries an aura of his presence
irradiating the world of stones
a Pointer of the Crest a measure set against
the Permanent Ice black sky
& marking limits of our presence

& by such means

merely fast-food notions of the truth
are exorcised by simple ceremony the rock
is taken from its very cracks/put out in circles
under the light moisture of the calming skies
in which the headlands half absent themselves

idea becomes journey journey idea on the surface of the
earth & stone/if you can walk in the world then clearly
it cannot be denied

'The leg thinks in distance, the arm in weights'
                    −ANDREW DUNCAN

he keeps a close watch on the movement of the blood
in the muscle of the heart
he keeps his eyes wide open on the line of sight
suggestion of the path to be trod/
the means by which it will be
made & by which that trace will be perceived
as imprint/
he is in the sculpture like Pollock is in the painting

but also bringing it right back home
held in the hand
a memory of that trace
pointing into the sky
you can look up there
to where
the stars may soon appear

it is an open secret

a ritual of quiet entry
into the prior & continuing existence of place some time
no vegetation no path no road no boat no crop no goat
no sheep/rock in the Little Pigeon River

drifting slowly out of Africa
walking is a time consuming process
in which the distance is continually marked
a ritual of conviction & care involving skill
a thin scarf protects the children from the sun

Inaugural Address (1979)

Good Day/you're in tune to If You're Going To Do It
Do It Alla Prima Time/

it's a Radio Babylon interference calling
a largesse of Delirius
more fundamental than America
ruddier than Silbury & more abused
greener than Mekonta &
mightier than the Wig in Wigan with a yellow in between/

Dreamier than the Kill in City
shinier than Krypton & more clear
more on top of it than Atlantis a
Blow Out on the Bauhaus
A Roll Over Old New Veau
A Knock Out on a Nico off the DD & D Co
A Granite Against Gropius/Toasting with The Hosting
No Touting for Bruno but
pouting & more tantalising than
Island Three the desiccated orifice of
The Woman with The Three of Everything she say
What on EARTH are Maltesers/what in THE WORLD
is a Power Tower/

A Cruising in a
3rd Century of The Decline
of Industrial Investment I & I for short The
Fantasia of The Plan Voisin Begat The Beaubourg
Glossier than La Ville Radieuse
& Sharper than Arcosanti The Architect
is The Invention of The Masterwork &
couldn't live without it/

Wrecking his Neck-Angle on the EuroStandard
we drift & mooch in the marinade of his metered Overspace
down on the Bogside Jesus & The Redevelopment Corporation

snicker into sight a fault in the beam-out from GPO Tower
back in Finance Capital/
neglected scabs of Venice Florence Rome Glasgow
flake under foot
on the black marble stairs of Milan Station

~

Inside The Riverside
Articulate Trace as Non-material form of Capital
blisters each side of your face with a blush
an intense blush blisters each side of your many faces
in the flux dance slab stance ba
lance of glittering felspar
the straitened moment speeding
in the ruinous curve of vinyl & circular dwelling
a cutting of deliberate gesture
in the passage of indelible act

~

Good-bye Savonarola Brunelleschi Alberti Bramante
Good-bye Dublin The Centre Pompidou The Guggenheim
Ghiberti's doors are the doors to the biggest bank
The Los Angeles County Museum of Modern Art The Hayward
The National Gallery "West" Berlin & Hello Tokyo
Good-bye the Monumental Fault & the Faulty Monumental
Great Fish-Knives of the Future Hello/Good-bye
Good-bye you fully automated cities that keep operating after we
        have all left
Good-bye computers transistors space-probes automation
        miniaturization acid & San Francisco
Good-bye the Marlborough Good-bye Sir Humphrey Gilbert/
not a room to be had in all of Broadacre
though you may get there
on The Old Straight Track
By the Rights of Orthogonal Planning/

Good-bye Auschwitz Hello Angkor Vat Pol
Pot Napoleon III Pinochet Pinocchio of Chairman Hua
Haussmann Mussolini Sant'Elia The God
Father of High Tech & he with no lustre on his
bite in the echo chain of Sardis the thatcher the carter
Teheran the Arc of the Shah
The Biggest McDonald's Advertisement In The World
Whose Cancer spreads easier than butter Kissinger
Rockefeller The Woman With The Three of Everything
Everything Terminates The Wedding
With Frozen InterContinental Rice/
Miniaturization of the Social Body
Into Occasional Table Arrangement
Micro-Explosion of the Thousands Transformer of Millions
peripheralized to the slotted sides of the votive Gold Heap
Market of Commodity Futures Miniaturized orgasm
of little yellow men spray from the planet edges
one by one
we drink & eat the sweat
& muscular steaks of Africa straight from the freezer
on Microwave Alert for The Republic
Sparta Miletus Periclean Athens:
The Acropolis Metropolis Necropolis Death Star Voiding
Hearthstones into 3D Vision Gelatine/

C'mon EveryBody/let me take your little pinkie
point your knees overhear
see me in the Arkle light of me anti-perspective altar back
shift your gear over here
get your fore-quarters into tune
& put them on this here blue plinth
Before your very stereoscopic vision
sky-junction Sky Junction
flux in sky junction Masterwork the flux of/
This is Sky Junction

Berlin Return (1983)

Craven Images

1

I like to dance so much & a kind of mania
conspicuously lures me on to your pointed hairless chest
but since here I am engrossed in the reading
of this here copy of *Sounds* & I am not Mechthild
only the punter with his meat on fire
outside the station in the fog I will swear
never to have seen you before in my life
when the Old Bill cruise by on their talking machines
matelots linger at the cab-rank I
carefully flick my second finger over the hard &
shiny folded notes in my shirt pocket
as the lull at the end of a lonely street
in the orange glare of the vast suburban night
holds me to the sluggish rocks of the pavement
your face in the shadowy shopfront at 3:00 a.m.
ain't exactly the ski patrol but then what with this
disaster area called my teeth like a roar of jacks
in a flashing orange search for a burst water-main
among the indeterminate commodities at the corner of the bar
Jackie Petersen dreaming over his amber sleeve of Brains
one immaculate black hoof over the brass rail
under the falling cloud of resin & chalk
passing from night to desk & desk to night
shoulder to shoulder with an immaculate new fish-tail
Where are the hatters of Luton? American devices
come round again like a thousand Chinese paper inventions
I would have liked to have been to Bucharest with you
Budapest anywhere taken all the boats the wagons-lits
mooch round all the bars gawping at all the young dudes
ate up all the food making for the Man in the Moon
crossing the Park in the soft purr of taxis
ah that sweet viola sound

her back is arched
& her breasts are bare
I feel a rose down
in her hair

the inimitable life of hotels
a rich display of feminist cactus in the lobby
lingering crows on the steps of Brompton Oratory
the poor animal life of the region we
will try the grand gesture the sag-arsed manner
the sculptors throw cat & rip off cock manner
tails the piece the hands of me manner
& up to a certain point manner
a couple of borzois on a leash manner

o baby what
a dog to be
in the Suck Age
of the bourgeoisie

perhaps I could finally bring myself to leave
your baleful pluralism my fingers
pause deliciously over sticky keys
as I hover over a faint icy rhythm
straps vibrating under your immortal propositions ideal
pedestrian on the King's Road
enraptured by the stare & cheek of very early Logic
another little Pils & pointless artless & frank
I get drunk without you
until the mixture degenerates & a bad odour
returns us to the Angel the harp player of the age
scraping his knuckles on the rough-cast ceiling
blood on the tambourine I sing
under my breath & my you're nervous
under the snow of a cold algebraic desire
an inkling of a kiss in the foyer

but in the calm of your bed in the late afternoon
there are these agreements of the body
the little pores in your back the gently lifting slats
parts of the outer city are atrocious
hatred of the meagre portion
even the bars are closed when we leave the cinema
it never stops no end in sight
till morning takes you home
here is your bed
be stupid beast & sleep
last of the occupants
who sadly scrape their feet

2

in the lines of the slipstream of an heroic express
coming in on the long curve eastwards into Cardiff
Atlantic rockas make their move a brazen cloud of
fiery smoke is lifting over GKN as we embark

& in the palace of globes a dazzling array of glasses
in various stages of depletion
& the sweet high tenor of the craic

under the rain under the sun & under the starry circus
the green sea rolling like an egg

3

black moleskin
tender pastures juniper & Coke

far from the underworld
green penetrates the sky levels

a glass of Volvic could have made me happy for ever

4

a glass of Avèze held me smiling vaguely in the grass
like a great lost wader
sad to have been a fighter & at what cost what times
& what a summer where are you now my little musics
mind you cowbells
                    make me sick
with misery & pain

                              ' . . . twenty times I have denied my heart
                              I am no longer able to rest'

I flew far in pursuit of your traces
une peinture une musique qui serait simplement voyou
the insanity of my legs the millions of my thighs
the tang of the pike in the mouth
a piece of chocolate sweating in the sun
like a very rare stamp in the middle of a banal collection
the bosses vacate the City at the hour of the illuminations
thousands of voices lift themselves up to heaven
in a velvet liaison with her boulevards
like love among the ants
the strawberries were ripening my ideas were turning blonde
the sky glazes over the purified volcanoes

5

The west side of the fishpond in the Jardin des Tuileries, looking across it & down the long terrace to the crepuscular distances of the Place du Carrousel. It is a bright sunny day. The usual scatter of public chairs has been cleared so that only three remain & these are placed very formally in a row looking out over the water. The carp or whatever, are jumping about all over the place. It is August 1970. There are two figures sitting quite still their backs & heads quite strikingly neat & similar. But the one on the left is Arthur. The other one is Douglas. The chair to his right is empty. "It's high time I was getting back to England you know, Douglas."

6

I was leaving, love on the platform
possessed of your greatness, o dear Thames
windows all lit up & rosy in the setting sun

This morning at 10:00 the Inter-City 125
will float me to Birmingham Stoke-on-Trent
but at the eleventh hour you grow sick at the rumour
                              in the back of the heart

likewise my craving for newsprint the smoke of small cigars
a proper slow burning characteristic of a superb condition
tumblers whirling downwards over shining rows of slate

your ideas were captivating & the wounds superb

as we rush out of Euston I turn & smile at the disappearing
                                                        grass

a dart has pierced to the centre of this alluring folly

Bad Thoughts

"You are unable to imagine that one day it will be possible for
    you to say hello to yourself to recognize yourself as a
        friend & to make a definitive peace of that
you remain surrendered to your alternatives
when it comes to tomorrow you are unable to recognize
    yesterday

the defunct days lean towards you with their images
from them you read off the inscription of your old outrages
& those yet to come tremble away into distant complaints

the scattered griefs fail to gather in the vicinity of where your
    heart has been
you have forgotten why you are sad
but you will know the hour where your sadness was born

tired of searching the night you will relish the day
she will nourish you with her light orchards
the trees of the night the trees of the day

the seasons turn in their balmy cycle
& you will not know what to say to their mild passage
it's a big chance you think it over

you cease to see yourself as a fit up for what is agreeable
exhausted by the winding distance covered by your staggering
    days
the lost homelands the rusted autumns

        & a fiery rose in the September sun
you will feel your body give way to its constituent parts
it will bear less resemblance to you than a rose-bush

the spring lies in wait for in order to prune
when the evening twilight falls on the deserted lane
you will not have any dread left in you

you may wish to cut yourself off from certain parts which you
        disapprove of
you would take a slice of this thing or that to offer up as a
        quarry
but when you rest on the restful breast of your lover

by her let yourself be carried as far as the border
where to be cancelled itself is to revoke all endings
accept yourself & your heritage from which you have been
        formed & passed from age to age

stay mysterious rather than be pure accept your
        multifariousness your pluralism
when you come finally to take leave of your youth
all the fallen dreams born of your very early childhood

shoot beside fresh jasmine
an adorable person comes together in your arms
at the charming little cross-roads where the day slopes

into the flat open country & the little hill expires
the implicit beauty of sacred places will be troubled for you
this restlessness will have put everything in question

& you will be subject to the craziest actions
but the road runs away from under your step the horizon never
        approaches
& you give yourself to this walking life to which the dust of the
        road attaches itself

Variations on 'Today Backwards'

for David Chaloner

1

Friday glitters toward lunch in parts
of cold wet trees
in the suburbs
of Africa
the sun
as high as it will go
in the birdless sky
before it drains
back of the darker gables

I listen to *The World At 1:00*
which hardens my heart & loosens my tongue

it will soon be 2:00 p.m. in the charcoal afternoon
the view from the page
anticipating foliage & a southerly breeze
to thaw the stippled white of Parker's Piece
a slightly grazed look
that tense immobility as of youthful hurt
stigmata reaching you from out the airwaves
of Radio Moscow
cancels the fantasy of invulnerability
from the inside out

nowhere else is quite the same today
franking these letters of dispersal

2

the week-end will go on in its petulant
fashion of glittering trees
like glasses of Pinot grigio
spread out toward Sunday
through several lunches
where dusk will come before tea
with its thoughts of Monday

an hour reading in the bath
& it's already 2:00 p.m. in the trembling day
where blue is like a shadow of itself
f-f-faulting the sky
& burying its insect life at your feet
a strictly timed immunity
beaming the voices of recreation into that staring sky
where they are strained of all local significance
into a new totality that sounds like parts of *Hymnen*

nowhere else was quite the same as today
floating between us on those signals

3

Saturday will burn up in the direction of Monday
soon enough its raw evening of pleasurable dusk
opening time soon come long gone before
the swifts get into town
as January fades into the big F

reading the *Star* in the space left after the round
then I harden my heart & polish my DMs
gather my shirt from the line & press it
sizzling black to the board
with pointed strokes
brush the old hair with Corimist a bit
before we hit the local ready to kill
an hour or two with gawping at the wealthy
strangers in the peer-glass an empty space
that fills up gradually with denim
or elusive unintelligible crackle

nowhere else will be quite the same tonight
as I lift my sleeve to you in the cadmium light

Two Sonnets

1

Living in a permanent band
                    strange as it seems
our musical dreams are here again.
For some reason you love yourself
but I'm right behind you
where I see the millions
                    leading from the back
I get the music
                    putting it on you
just a little grey light to read you by
5:30 a.m. under the sheets
                    lobbies apart.

                    In the midst of this shy erotic panic
great chunks of falling masonry
that look like love

& yet "Can anyone really be doing this?"

I hold back the final word
silent in the face of what I see

2

a cry carries over from an obscure
                              part of the street
hours & hours go by, then
                        strange as it seems
our musical dream is here again
closing the frontdoor after itself

I know you will enter the room in 25 seconds
a freesia or two in your green lapel
the storm in the chimney shaking
                            voracious
for the books
              you read last summer, this winter
I tear into your heart as though for the first time

a shining world of metal & stone
                          at your throat
a bright mocking noise & I love you *con molto furioso*
bringing you
            metal of a lower order
to bite into the ice of this approaching festival
where laughter & lamplight
                        catch at the livid skin

After Satie, a Concert, 13 June 1972, on the Beach, Aldeburgh

this is my heart that is balancing here

but there is only a slight dizziness

what little feet it has
will it want
to come back to my breast

(can you hear the rabbit singing
the nightingale in her burrow
the owl suckling her young)

Do be careful lady

Your lover is very near

he is holding his heart with both hands
but you don't even notice

The ocean is vast madame.
At least, it's extremely deep

Look at the dear old waves.
They are filled with water
Don't go so near, you'll get completely drenched

The octopus is in his lair.
He amuses himself with a little crab
He catches her
but she goes down the wrong way
Haggard, he stands on his toes
& drinks a glass of bourbon in order to recover.
The drink does him a lot of good & changes his ideas

A Page

Shaven to the bone as a sign of respect for your powerful charm, I stand near the edge but you don't even notice. We say nice things to each other, modern things, like in a Jean Rhys story, like "Don't you love me?" Look that's my heart you've got there. Excuse my slight dizziness but I was wondering if I could have it back? Is this the ambulance or the way to the hot dog stand? Later I return to my lair & amuse myself with a little dressed crab & a half-bottle of hock, some of which goes down the wrong way & makes me cough. I drink a glass of malt in order to recover. The drink does me a lot of good & changes my ideas. Like, you don't keep Sutton's Summerday Lawn Seed in the bedroom, you keep it in the garden shed. You didn't know? Do you think you'd have done anything different if you had known? Seaweed. Elastic vanities. "Being without you is hard work, it tires me out."

Karol in Tunisia

1

Did he imagine the difficulties of the road he wanted to follow when he was dreaming of his first compositions, when he was writing operettas which he presented with the aid of his cousins in his native village out on the huge Ukrainian steppes?

A poetry of yellowing pages, the charm of the eyes of the young Scriabin, a certain grace, a lightness of texture, there is no knowing how his powers would have developed if it had not been for the friends he made in Warsaw.

2

It is almost March again. I have the impression that some little boxes with musical valves have opened inside me

      like a boy, a switch cut from the fields,
    striped matelot undershirt, white open collar,
        the air is moving the branches over my head,
      I am listening to its music, it
does not matter if from time to time some facetious &
    cynical little creature gives us a small bite
or that we are so seldom alone that instead of talking
    we make signs to each other

      the river glints a harmony
      sensitive, nervous & not invariably accurate,
      in Zakopane, there you can really be alone,
      wanting to be with friends, on the veranda,
      the double tones, the pasture bells,
      dancing a new mazurka

3

Before & long after Chopin there was a complete & prolonged silence. Oh Karol!

After Francis Amunatégui

The appearance
of a hot sausage
with its salad
of potatoes in oil
can leave nobody
indifferent . . .

it is pure, it
precludes
all sentimentality,
it is
the Truth

Bye Bye Blackbird

for Douglas Oliver

over the clay-laden estuary a
soft grey light comes sneaking
my heart away it is the spirit of Colne Spring

& all along the shoreline an oyster-catcher
dips & bobs a splashing blur of black & white
against the easterner

curlews ghosting by a little above the fleet
fly our souls out of perversity

Brightlingsea has grown where it is the sepia
gaff-rigged sails of the smacks manoeuvre away

into the Dutch hinterspace beyond Mersea Island a rich
alluvium gets itself laid over years we mooch along

towards a frith
dreaming of sprats & opals

Song

after Richard Long & Johnny Cash

for an hour I walk a line to you
then mark the distance on a map

each of the following days
I walk the line & the sculpture becomes

slower & slower from day to day,
day to night, day night day,

till Wednesday moving slow the train rolls in
& you come walking out

Wearing My Little Blue T-Shirt Again

1

a leaf of the vine
wraps the fruit of the ewe
in the calm of the public gardens at le midi
with the bread & the wine
the chance of weathering the afternoon
like a thread of white cotton in the breeze

2

on the dark side of the room
foliage touches the window
a skirt trails on the stairs

under the single lamp
your eyes are transparent
& hold the attention
like a tiny glass
of colourless liquid

3

like
the violet
   puts out
& takes

   the sun
my nose
is thrust
into the sky

& takes a look
at what is there

the wet
earth
offering
night

One for Rolf

in the grey-green morning rain a displaced April
air in May, the breath & motion of our life
never a last thing, we hold to the page & the voice,
the lighter quality that sometimes flickers in this green,
a correspondence of approach
hidden beneath a difference of appearances,
beyond which we expire like the breeze at evening

(the struggle for what is light
in what is dark

shone to advantage
in our backyard

when there's someone I like in the room
I don't need to think everything's funny

I make another cup of coffee
& everything is OK

"Speed" sys Ed "is not necessarily fast"

Traffic lights, tall
lamp-standards, thin trees,   WALK,
so I walk, writing myself into a new place
where the dream I have in my head each day
becomes a new compilation of existence

langsam langsam
                    getting to know the view up front there is
a mirror on the plane – me too

a gentle rain
steadies down over the city

the permanent way
shines

in the pale evening light

There has been the slightest loss of attention

I wouldn't have known what to say
if my life depended on it

it was as if the news had turned into the day
or the day had turned into the news saying oh no

but it's quieter here at the back
away from the street
& I haven't a line in my head that could
sound like a thought of Hölderlin

ZACK! ZACK!
there has been an accident in my life o my life

2:35 p.m.   outside the
in Cologne   AUTOBAD

     no trees to speak of

it's stopped raining, wide pools
spread over the cobbles,
pick up the silvery grey light

Three postcards:

a big square of pink blossom
climbing twin spires
above the wavy Rhine

a big black fuzzy shape
is heading through the air
straight for the Dom Hotel

a big yellow articulated tram
clangs by on the Rudolfplatz
ONKO KAFFEE ONKO KAFFEE

torso on the grass
                    discarded   DONT
shirts   WALK
        left hanging to dry
                        in the bathroom
                    all day long
                    the shadow trickling
                across the road
                            to the framehouse

                        EXIT
                            ing

                        on the wing

in the new good morning day
Andrew looks out his window
at his back-yard in Lewes
& sees the level light drawn to the earth, love
of the creatures
                    shining from the haunts of memory again
like the dream I have in my head each day
where you are, partly, but also on the outside
your sense of the zeitgeist never very far away

        at the airport
        at the airport terminal
        at the radio

        at the toast
        at the rickety buildings in the street
        at the typewriter:

                    abfahren

the history of your life
a pagination of existence in which I partly live
a slow exposure to the radiance left by you

by you & all you others

 one day   tomorrow

just like any other day that's ever been & it's
morning again in our green back-yard
after a night of no-dream dreaming & I
hear you say "I am still living in the same world
since I am born"
                  & Ted, I hear him
read the words "Tomorrow you die"
& me, I say
                  "Are you kidding? See you later!"

Narrative Graffiti

> 1956–57 works in the fields; 1957–60 recovery
> from working in the fields
> JOSEPH BEUYS

> I am also my own medium
> DAVID BOWIE

... our acknowledgement
of the world, the variousness of that response,
mantelshelf postcards, so many people leaving town,
street-air, flutter of curtains, what they are
going in for, body & soul, it's just that

sometimes you feel you must get out in the light
your head alive & glowing, a reply
to the lobster or a Moon solo
or the dear old stars stream by
an open window – the sky, the great sky –
which holds me in suspense

she gave him ten o'clock breakfast
the tower rang
she wrote his song

& walking near the kerb
the black sky
shines over everything with rain

your arm no longer trembles
                                 when
cooking in the vast well you

call my name
                I walk on back

stuttering
bragging

cold perfunctory official
she'll come she'll go

she'll lay belief on you
& when her benevolent mood returns

she might go out again

eating a body
            from day to day
small fires
            my mouth
moving over
& when the clothes are strewn
                        don't
leave me to the moths

                  (oh Johnny
to feel your hands
in my hair

if you don't want to eat me
you can eat
somebody else

in a pink one-piece costume
uncaring for the grains of sand
entangled in your drying hair you sprawl
in hesitant languor
at the feet of someone who cares for you
beneath the hurtling sun
while disparate trees
like tufts of soft green hair
wave invitingly from the hotel garden

John Wilkinson's photo

so you take the sky, the stars really aren't
that far away
              & it's mainly a business of nerve
as you negotiate the street

"Is this the ambulance
or the way to the hot dog stand?"

I use your perfume which makes me think
you're here in the night but don't worry
if I break guitars I break guitars
because I like them I usually break them
when they're at their best

listening
        (the old fart listening

again & again

        The High Numbers

& still not able to decide

a day in the fields

two sheepdogs cross in & out
the passing shadow
                the clouds drift
over the hill with the storm
not a line in my head that could sound like a
thought of Hölderlin
the strain of being is killing us both
but together we will try
to raise the spirit of the earth
& move the rolling sky

four excessive moves I made today

1. Ate too much lunch

2. Ate too little dinner

3. Talked too much

4. Retired sober

a day in the mountains

after the last sound fades
a power will ride
where the river ebbs then turns again
to meet the Severn & the sea
                              Dunkery
                  miles & miles
away across the Channel
                        a morose bulk
in the shimmering air of the planet
though gales bring on
a sidelong yellow sober light
                        diffusing day

you've just come back
I definitely love you

After Christopher Wood

it would be ordinary enough to live
in a room that balanced above

the sea's implied presence
a soft draught of light taken in

by the half-open lips of pale green shutters
quenching the tender places

left in the flesh of the mouth

caused of a recurring breathlessness
caused of living in low places

& we could relax into that thing
we vaguely call life whatever
the shade of dress in which it might present itself

& we could sprawl on a white bedcover
reading the *Lives of the Poets*
provided – & this indeed would be a provision of
our existence – that we brought nothing
mean or sordid into that place by virtue
of our mutually ridiculous appetites
whereby we are able to lose each other up to the last moment
when your fingers catch at my lips in a smile
& we do become dwellers in that glittering place
the towels white with orange borders
a kind of mortal incompatibility

Cambridge

the rain in its new edition of daily menace
continues to flap rags of black sky over the gables
a shout carries over from the end of the street
where are the dear old stars? you smile
it's getting very near to six o'clock in all those places
I said I'd never go again & then did as if I'd never
even forgotten where friendly academic barflies
laugh & sulk interestingly
creatures of an easy recognition
with carved intelligence & murder in their hearts
the sweetish smell of Fatimas poison the air
& clamorous voices make you want to climb the wall
& gnaw your way across the ceiling
                                            meanwhile
my little sweetheart of the steppes your laugh
brings light to me as the otherwise silent house
occasionally sways in a gust the telephone
obdurate & yellow on the blue rug
the rising gale now pulling the whole room
apart at the seams as you do your clothes
to big applause for Little Feat
we brace ourselves for what we each deserve
in dreary September & I think about my friends
who are not here the light these days giving
a faint glint of melancholic languor
to the wild traceries of honeysuckle in the
garden across the street a carnal resonant air
rasping a spray of rusty water from
chuting under the eaves something goes pop in my eyes
what's that tragic fringe up around the edge of
the ragged beeches out the back? you cry
for a while & then look exquisite & vicious
there'll never ever be I just couldn't be
anyone else but you

Chute de Pierres

looking for a new geological disposition
the grey eyes in the white face rock on
in the opalescence of an afternoon in middle May
wrestling with the ambiguities of a stony pallor
as if they were markers on the route carrossable
on a descent to the city of Toulouse where
to the accompaniment of bagpipes the moon concedes me
artisan of your daily beauty & we rise surrounded
by a crowd of petty doubts like a shower of grape pips
on arrival at 'Lafayette Railroad' it will be time for
breaking the ice for the martinis which will open up a
little wicker gate where as far as Engels is concerned
an axe in the hand at least gives you a free foot
to walk about with you don't get that
back to nature feeling in the chalkland though
you simply exist in the middle of an excavation
a manufactory of flint implements the resort
of archaeological enthusiasts real amateurs
dropping in & out above the floorstone

Sister Midnight

stuttering rain at the window
early in autumn your breast
loosed from its hold
the caprice of your lifting thighs
the serious depth to your smile
I seem made of insubstantial elements like a leaf
the otherwise silent house occasionally sways
two blocks away the river seeps from lock to lock
the telephone obdurate & yellow against the blue rug
the gale now pulling the whole room apart at the seams
hungover leaves fill up the dusty often
can't do anything at all at other times
you just don't care at all you try it
your own way her face a little blue that shaky
girl with the shaky hand can't hold the pen
too weak for the desk the lower chair
the lower sky hurry by on the pavement outside
everything slipping away with the day
which is closing in on itself at 3:58 the sky
all lit up between a crack in the buildings
& under those clouds lie the chimneys
decorated with a fretwork of little birds
& large grey washes of sky over the gables

the bell rings but I refuse to answer
I might have been a painter but there was an accident
in my life right down the line of a fierce fatigue
replete with overcoats my cherry which is why it is worst
when you have forgotten the mayonnaise remember
I told you there'd be something funny about it she said
like her potatoes of lead, flash flash, alas a
cold pallor has overcome my scrotal sac
in the sharp gusts of autumn in all those places
I said I'd never go again & then did

as if I'd never even forgotten
                         meanwhile
your head my little sweetheart of the steppes
don't hesitate grab the momentum while the going's good
sink to your knees beside the yellow sofa
take him between the folds of my bright magenta wraparound
the bright glossy oval of a knee & remarkable vest
rippling up over my becoming
the casual spectator of hoydens in the sharp grass of the park
steam rises from the coffee cups
the wine splashes into the little glass
a vigorous red in keeping with the tone
of all that battles to be without my arm
oh my arm in this smallest minute where I enter your name
for the aim of the race do you know
there are certain sounds which tear at my liver
like a cat at its matted fur & a certain
absence of detail has for the first time
featured in my life tightening my collar
& lurking near the black marble of Italian headstones
shining back at the bright little windows of the local
do-it-yourself shops in the rising morning
like a sickness that imprisons the heart in a fettered glove
& now I recognize your great talent as a member of the
human race as the peasant offers me the plastic salt-box
& I look around for the snuff of the father
painted in green & embroidered in my vest
as a text for my meditations

outside the window the trees move in the night
your grand desire rises in my throat & my heart
pulses on into its thirty-sixth year like an indifferent
steam-engine while milky tea embalms the organ
a woman feels very cold around the buttocks
once in a while & yet your laugh brings light to me
cause you're the first good man I've found
pressing the glossy black embellishments to the hand

under the gentle curtain imagery of the gasfire & the
dusty smell of old red velvet cinema seats
               but still this hanging over
               of the female in the man
               means maybe
               rather than
& that's not the end but a beginning like when
you can't turn the key any further in the sardine can
& all along the edge of the skyline
the last green cringe of daylight
drops like a plate to the ground

Shakin All Over

dip your head in the basin & go
walking the early morning streets late March rotting
from the inside out leather under
dog-tooth green check tweed
lathering the aching in the rib-cage just got to be
got up & gone I'm not turning away I'm
not looking down I'm puzzling over
the influence of the Stickies I
freely enter your special unit I
don't look down
light drapes flap at the covered windows
touch at the hairs at the back of the hand
the shackling of trucks in the sidings rattle of
curtain rings & soon I hear that crazy fluttering sound
cut through an otherwise absolutely silent room
it's the undertones
of your vibration rattle of pink noise
the poise with which you set your arm alight
our mutual pride &
randomly chosen limited isolation

oh baby what a place to be to disregard
the giant hoard of wounds this tress
in the creaking of copper ear-rings
strands pins & hair-slides & drinking Black Bush
a wave of dark air rolls through the barley
& then you can recall it all &
jet discs rattle as you walk
close to the shifting metacentre
that stripe in your wrist where
the heat is still fresh &
reckless of the edge your face as pale as
quartz or gypsum you're turning backwards
to a new scene as the lozenge dissolves into

crossover & he leisters the jumping thigh
with whatever comes to hand a beer-can amber or zip
the flax caught in the teeth of the comb
& she cries out for once & for all
churning the mud in the pool

                              & later
in the studded augury of bar-tables in the Midland
the immediate future appears strictly female there
will be somebody to talk to & I like to look at you
without somebody watching over us happy &
glorious & even under close escort
the narrow band of pouncing
will be hidden in the skin
                              & we'll be
lapping up a sleek pony
eye rolling over a speckled back zigzag
the stun-shot sways you as you stay on top
they say you'll never be free
but give me your hand here
under the duress of sliding straps
the tang of the white bush
the linen spattered with honey & lager
the dawn spouting with little birds & pressing
a shoulder-blade to the mattress
& there's not so much as a bit of boiling pig
left to be eaten the coverlet hoods you
squinting into the sunlight the talk
twirls at your throat & your hard green
is painted with flashing white
emulsion disinfectant as you apply an orange
towel to the stomach the neck the
perforated magma warm & moist & groaning

Poem for Bruce McLean (1983)

"the carp in its dark pool
shadows the salmon of memory

under the feinting willow
their burnished scales

splashed by moon & stars
& violet petals

breaking through
these creatures turn

& arc in grace
against the blue

the rush of air
& flow of darkness

at the rim
the paler branches quiver

cascade lit
the mossy stone

& wavering lip
the silent fishes

turn again & glow
in long anticipation

as the veils of polythene are rent
in the temple

the canvas shudders
the flank of a horse

at the entry
the uncertain sky

so soon your eye will see the surface
in the depths of things

the rush of energy
& very early light of day

out of the cold of the lonely street
where the pain is dislodged
like an old triangle
in the field of the indeterminate
heads build to grey
modelled from single quick gestures of the hand the arm

the absolutely confident hand
tries out a few different pieces of body furniture

the green lips of certain women deny all appetite
as the hands of the others clench & point & smear

the mouth in the mirror receives its anointment
as the glass slides away
as the index signals 1

& the arrows of a bland libido
search out the goblets of a chunky wrist
the supremely confident hand chin attention
ways of arranging a boiled egg in its elegant cup
& I begin to know you as your luscious hair
drips into this containment

as your forehead turns into the room
obscures your eye in its elegant cup
a lick of red escapes me

the utterly direct basilisk stare
offset by the fact that one of its eyes
seeks out a third

so you give me touch sight & sound
the egg-cup becomes an ear-ring
& I feel happy again to be writing this

we live so much by the eye
but the ear's an organ too
which sticks out neatly from the side of your head
& carries an earnest of desire in the ring that dangles there

the left eye on her chin
the right eye swerved to take the light
that shines from his

the fish the triangular passage of despair
as the down stands on the nape of the small of your back

one eye on hers
the other swerved to take the light
that shines from his

over the heads at the pictures
that shafting silvery light is here again

softly smouldering postponable lust

the beam in your eye
the ever present assassin
the yellow lunula

like the bell signalling the start of another day at school
when we were very young & green

white man turning grey against the reds
above them the stars
the satellites the sausages
closer to home a tasty finger or a
knuckle sandwich
coming in from the side on a body swerve from somewhere else
the intruder in the arm of yourself
is it his arm or her arm or yourn
where shall I place this arm
not to put too fine a point upon it the fingernails
are edged in black right down to the flux link
the grip a little infirm as perhaps it should be
an envelope addressing itself
to the How Firm Handshake Question
keeping a careful eye on the studded wrist
your lovely breast adrip with paint beside itself

all this has been plunging forward through the week
the lamp burning in daylight

in the city
where your strong neck
merges with the line of your head
& your tough little mouth
very seldom falters

in the face of those other lips
which pose like satisfied anemones
those hands like gauntlets strike me
pink against that grey

but that'll be the day
a flicker of the country in the bar
blows in across the threshold of the open door
& your love was fairly near me too

oh probably on Sunday mornings as we lay in bed reading
the reviews & sipping cold coffee
even though it was moving off in the direction
in which it was always free floating

did you really think I'd ever stop

in the gallery your thoughts sometimes turn to such matters
as they do to cups of tea or chocolate rolls
which I never eat

but the writing's on the wall
you fill the width
before it suddenly takes off to reappear later
further down

by the set of their shoulders you shall know them
these have been in the gym at least three times this week
while these others have lingered over lunch
& yours are nowhere around as yet

is there a barstool around here somewhere
how do your shoulders feel after encountering hers

how the weather changes at our backs

the aching palm of the hand no sooner touches the chin
when suddenly there's a flurry of snow at the window

a breakfast scene at 6:00 with greasy hair
a mean sideburn interleaves
the shining layers of the surface of the globe

an aquiline nose or two never did anybody any harm
I reassure myself

such a delicate neck
eyebrows diminished to the point of oblivion
the further we got from the fields
the more it became a set piece face to match the day
a forehead like a rabbit brow in
version to the self

a blank erotic mouth sings the history of lack
as you ponderously scratch the left side of your neck
with your right hand

these others shriek attention
of an unseen crowd of
Rowlandson grotesques

the hennaed hair sways
to a thousand synthetic kisses

emerging from the pits
in a swirl of conviviality
white man turning grey against the stars the reds
blue neon spiral in
shiny blackstuff

you look into her eyes her teeth her chin
like a well-muscled dentist on vacation the hero
surrounded by her so-called friends
you look up you look down
she turns her hip upon the Li-lo

soaked in the smell of Ambre Solaire the heads move
to place the particle of food into your mouth
the finger the bratwurst
hesitation before nose installation

are you there mon ami

yes I'm scratching my chin

the bathers with their green & orange towels
running on the darkened beach
buttocks & nipples all aglow
the shadowy armpits

earlier in the day
sun burning in the pool
the well-fed swimmers
tell each other things behind their hands

the way you stroke your nose
the way you swing off key
your hat your rod your staff descending

the finger extends from a green lip
& twirls a hat around the index

silent in court
& rank in the treads

this one holds his head in his hand
this one holds his hands akimbo
in readiness for whatever fate awaits him

as the fork the stick the bicycle wheel
contend the yellow
frieze along the lilac stairs

a collection of party hats
grieve over their departed innocents

auf der Mauer steht mit gelber Kreide

they want culture war
sidelong glances & the bland determined stare
a splendid neck-tie in the company of friends
transcends the category of ridiculous garment

what comfort in that tiny window
to pay the supreme penalty
his grey trouserless legs
swinging among the assembled heads

he who wrote it watches forever at the gate

o gorgeous neck-tie in das Meer
where the figures wait
to be towed away

a long violet glove
touches the painted lips with velvet

yucca yucca wonder bar
detachable collar & tie

back to the stone
back to the strong arms of the man you love

those looks of hers which measure the depths of something

you pass above the cloud of senses
you pass along the crowd of sense

like a chisel along a previously silent block of gritstone
pain is just the memory of a higher future or a severed past

the feathered dancer in the sky at night
tells me something behind the hand of the clock

the shadow in the frame of light from the projector
drinking Coke from a gleaming phantom

no contest Mr

then come what may
we'll eat today

& look at her & her
tomorrow

a gestural piece of lino escapes from another work

as you walk the neon night
in a flash of red

who smiles on you
above the rolling wheels of headlit cars

the heads in the café bars encroach upon your dreams
at dawn the lingering smile you never met
& never was the Laura of your dreams

the last touch of warmth at her breast before you left

I want to kiss your ochre lips
reach out for the curve at the top of your inner thigh

what aching countenance what loving smiles
what anxious caring eyes

offset by shaven napes
white turning grey over you

I say no to all your luxury
the greatest luxury of all

their heads attired in orange glories
refraining from absolute devastation
they do look down

tremble beneath that steady gaze
& rise to her turning away
to the faint sound of her bangled wrist
the darker side of you

feel a little cold the chink of light
prise open the lower edge of sky
at the tops of the concrete

miles & miles & miles away
the yellow stripe
as night surrenders to the dawn

above the empyrean
gyration of yellow dancers
pale shadows of our former selves
their looks are bigger than all of you

John I was only dancing
green electricity & rock
in the naked happiness of your loving arms

blue flashes lead us forward through the encircling gloom

& you are standing there in the gallery which is
after all is said & done a
very nice place to put pictures &
wondering about the creases & folds which inevitably appear
in your new corduroy trousers mere mortals
they fold you up like perfect movement
in the strategy of the brush the hand the arm
no more crossing out

the second crossing out supersedes the first crossing out
we bow in awe their heads look down
& measure the depths of something
they've got it taped the lines the angles the arrows
the unwritten rules they
don't take notes they are beyond gravity
they are the object of a loss of self-attention
body & fantastic solo runners gymnasts o danseuses
the long yellow beam of the spotlight
in the view from the gods
as the smoke curls up from the pit from the stalls
you smile in your solitude & isolation in the sky
washing the dust of each day's journey from your face

Lines for Richard Long (1988)

somewhere in England in 1967
a line is made by walking in the green
& a window opens like a door on Clifton Down

those were the days as now
the south-west wind brings elevation of the broken cloud
dispelling the milky film of Cambridge habit
from the eastern sky a day for acoustic guitar

the touch of weather on these shiny roof-tops
is of no immediate importance or utility
the countless days the countless stones continue

all that language all that writing
indelible distance we travel us to

still holding the line still walking the line
at variable speeds not necessarily fast

a day a night forever all that making it
can say or do

& as the sun-wheel turns over Crickley
high into Monmouthshire

the spokes aflare
with a light dusting of lime

Turf Circle

a north wind moves over the winter sky-line

in opening cloud
the hesitation of the stars

an echo in the hollow

in the Bell Pool
the blue salmon

a clear leap to Usk

the walker rest
by the harbour wall
on the isle of Mona
that pleasant crossing-place

paddle & breaker
gull & wave

"oh pigling you were my sole companion in the forest

I walked from Kilconnell along the Cliffs of Moher & down into Fisherstreet & I came to the *Circle in Ireland* just as you said it was quite unchanged save for the flowers growing in the cracks on the flat fissured limestone beds above the sea & the Aran Islands below Connemara & the Twelve Pins across the bay to the north-west the power of The Burren away at the back the changing skies above & the Cliffs to the south

Later sailing into Cill Rónáin from Ros an Mhíl I recognised the north-west landfall of Inishmaan & thought to look for the *Stones* toward the southernmost coast of Inishmore the following day. The next morning reading T. Robinson's map of the islands I found the work to be clearly indicated & so I walked out along to the old tower & down to the field of stones where many of yours still plainly stand pointing back across the Sound & through the islands back to the *Circle* & Clare

the grey colour of a pear
in the quiet light of the kitchen
the glittering branches at the window

the force of the hearth breaks out
invoking name & lineage

it's a good step
that will continue to the end without arriving

When you take up your pack & go
to the remote & desert places of the Earth
your path is a watercourse
or a torrent on the slope

the walker in summer-time on slanting ground
in a robe of vapour

by night there will be shelter
in the hollow & the cleft

I was a walker in earth before I was proficient in learning
catching the deep night & dawn divide
the line of the curling wave on the extended shore

now the leg thinks in distance & the arm in weight

CLOUD SUN CLOUD THUNDER CLOUD HAIL RAIN SUN

Saturday lime Sunday oak & quick-thorn
the place of the little drop & the length of the Avon
when it fills when it overflows
when it disappears in a dark thicket
quick sunlight between clouds

& from above the tops of the whirling trees
measure the veil of the drops in the air
at the width of the river's mouth
when the sea is turning round

the words in the book & the book in its beginning

The Ghost of Jimi Hendrix
at Stokesay Castle (1988)

it's 1983 & purple shoes are dancing
on a whiff of fading sandalwood

there's a new guitar in town
free & running in the English style

where each one do the monkey
under a soporific eastern sky

all but indifference

the real attachment
illogicality compromise & cant

on a one-way ticket to London

you may then return to America
as if you were English yourself

~

What is this haze all round
don't know if I'm going up or going down
lately things just do not seem the same

she'll be falling in love in a second
the way I've always known

it is fitting that at Ludlow
we fall upon the allure of Plumpton Place
shining from the cover of Aslet's book
the last country house that singularity
the photograph that moves a
sheen evocative of Twyn Bell in 1967

these things happen

The Experience was an English act
but the English house is not one building

all that timber work comes out of Stokesay
Argentan

& doubles back
Le Bois des Moutiers

elemental my dear Hudson

you can't believe everything you see & hear can you
the old heroes of desire sleeping where Handel slept
it's a long way from the surf
& the sign for victory equals peace
the River Onny & its mood of total calm

when you're dead you're made for life

the north tower roof
worn at a rakish angle like a new guitar

all those little things he do with his hair
the flash elusive grace

a scavenger of mud
I do respect my other
tour of purple haze
where broken limbs
& cardboard fires burn

the Port-O-San man
with one son here
another in the DMZ

the face of a boy

the cave of despair

barbwire sweetheart it's a long way from home
but I'm right there in your picture-frame in black & white
we fight for what we love not are
but now my signal turn from green to red
Mau Mau Jimi let them laugh
we love you forever you big dope

Local (1990)

the early morning sky across the lough
the very early light of day
a little cognac

a shining drop on the golden skin
mahogany amber chenille
table & curtain

swallow an olive

no it's not that autumn scene you love
the tiny clouds you've been attentive to
the lamplit corner of the roof

it's spring & a child in red smocking
walks unsteadily near the byre
her name is Róisín

pale as the early morning trees
a northern air
warms to the touch of sudden eyes

a seasonal delay

no longer falters at the margin
doorstep & window
work like a charm

the hand at ease at the white vellum
the rain soft in the hedgerow
dark & calm

drifting smoke as the coals are lit along the street
high walls a stone of steady grey
blue lustre of wet slate

curling o'er the flickering heart
a voice outside
the open path

soon it will be time enough to eat
a quiet beer
a slice of soda bread

back to the big room still as it was
a ready measure
for the level trace

the vast tumultuous heaven
off-white & blue
rears overhead

it does that a lot we take no notice
another tractor rolling by
in the big wide hills

a sunlit moment at your fingernail
a cup of milky tea
before it all shuts down again

or the evening breaks into a glow
a call to the bar
inviting dry but mellow

after the whirling passage of the sun
the silent company
at rest awhile now work is done

Dreaming Flesh (1991)

For the Safety of Lovers

I can & do lie down with you amidst the venomous,
charmed & safeguarded against all
harm in the unregarded instant, the
reciprocation that all
lovers dwell in, as fond of
watching the pale light start &
fade in the other's skin
as of trying to enter it
entirely. Even lying down where I know
poisons must inflame
my pores & do, somewhere,
the elbow say, the rash
blisters out. Oh what a
great distance off
from the inviolable &
imaginary self.

The Conversation

Snowdon is falling apart. You can't walk upright now
along the ridge beyond Crib Goch toward the Pinnacles
the Zig Zags are held together with wire mesh
& climbers wearing Vibrams should be careful everywhere
as everywhere is very slippery in the rain

(boggy ground, boulders, the derelict sheepfold yes but
the tricky bit is almost vertical all the way
so Mr Poucher can no longer be retained on trips like this
I'm sorry to say!

It's the 19th of August 1982, stepping on quartz
the power quietly rising through my left vibram
the horizon opening like a door, 600 feet to go.
I could show you in a word if I wanted to

but I look up in complete detachment
the taste of copper pennies beginning to abate
among the mysteries of love & hate

this great volcanic frame of things in all
the revolutionary hope & practices
of women & of men does not remain unchanged
it too has its faults through which an exile voice can sing

& driving through the rain from Welshpool
over the mountain into Bala
I'm not ashamed to think of might have been despite myself
which marks a stage of progress
on fixing on what was at least
& wonder for just how much I am to answer
having to stop & stop again to write

If there is always memory in working-class life
it is because things are always being taken away the head
spinning from day to night with little accidents

& love's the chief the drug
as Bryan Ferry sings
                              that gone
we fall to gravel beneath the span
& 7 burdens which it brings of
stupefying duties & degrading cares
labour poverty debt disease & grief no single call
received today oh yes the waste & crass stupidity
continual strife at work & in the street
the want of pleasure & repose
& all that drinks away the sustenance of choice

I see you in the daily mirror cooking for others
a softening countenance of delicate desire
lingers like the choice of all the world,
is it raining in New York on 5th Avenue

"du bist Maria und du bist meine Frau"

to say nothing of you Jeremy when you leaf
your pages to that summer & have before you
all we make of what we are when every day
gave some new sense of strengthening regard for common
            things
& all the land gave up a breath of gentler touch
but for the undertow of darkness
in the phones

hanging by unseen fissures in the grey & slippery rock
held buoyant by the streaming wind & rain
we live so much by the eye & yet
the ear's an organ too

keep looking up!
with what strange utterance does the rushing air
blow through my floating head the sky & motion of the cloud
no light above the level of the mist & biting hail
glimpse of a familiar figure by the brook

I see the millions I catch the language
which is the world of all of us
this only place in which we find our happiness or not at all
the end

From Pass to Pass

by the fringe
of skin & hide
in late July

step off the tarmac & go
with pack & stick
& a box of Swan

the stones do tell
of every place & hand

oh trace the journey
on a map

the pale green wood

landfall of island
or peninsula

a clearing in the forest

Havana Moon

at the first sip

the splash of
broken jug or bowl

the curl of the wave

the light touch of rain

Spanish Point

the first wave of morning
spreads over the sand

a bicycle
& the hoe at work in the open field

the air trembles
at the grey sky-line

the hidden act of lifting
in the pale front of Atlantic space

LUNDY

FASTNET

SHANNON

Song

after Friedrich & Goethe

on Pen y Fan a
thousand times I stand
reclining on my staff
& gazing down the valley

then I follow the grazing sheep
& the dog looks after them
I find myself down there but how
I scarcely can tell

the meadow is full of
delicate flowers I
take without knowing
where I shall give

in rain & storm & gale
I linger under the tree
but the door stays shut
& all desire

a rainbow risen
above a distant house
but she doesn't live there anymore
she's far from

the land of my fathers
perhaps even over the sea
move on then shepherd move over
so soon the walker must be

After Rilke: December

& night & the rolling wheels of the column of the army
trailing in along the park.
He looked up & glanced at her across the instrument
while still continuing to play.

It was almost like looking in a mirror
so very full of his own young features
& knowing his sadness deluding beautiful
& more compelling with every note.

But instantly that seemed to fade.
She stood as if with effort in the window-bay
& held her heart for all its beating.

The sound gave way. Outside it blew afresh
& on the dressing-table strangely foreign
the black shako with the death's head.

A Letter to Paul

the head turning, a red cavity with a dark place.

The arrows only go to show, between ourselves, that the plaster gave me a fright. The door ajar with a sinister glare, the frame askew with a feathery glow. Are you there where I think you are?

The protective hand, fume of burning hemp, the northern air, occlusion of line.

Get me a drink more powerful than dreams where the separate kiss & walk away. Somewhere on earth, Saint Ives perhaps. Being & doing nothing together, lacking a raincoat of sufficient poise for the local arbiters of taste, a marginal spectre. The pigment springs alive from the frosted earth.

Do you have an address for Bobby Walker? All this bacon is too much, my daughter said between shadows of black satin.

The air flows in the trench of Ross Street gathering the rubbish in its current. I hope to visit Georgiana before they close the frontier. It can be done. Love, John.

After Picasso

that was our bedroom
you see my shadow

I had just moved away
from the window you see

my shadow & the sunlight
falling across the bed

do you see the toy cart on the chest of drawers
& the little vase on the mantel

they came from Sicily
they're still in the house

Polka

now we go
you & I

like a bayleaf
in the sky

& the other bit
that I forget

vivid

later I stopped work
after two years flat out

& got flat out
& you came back

into my head
going flat out

that old
jingle jangle

never stop

ever loving
Johnny

stand in a queue
stand in a ring

bounce on the floor
& howl & sing

Nocturnal

the hidden story a spot of blood in the snow on Geifas
the hidden song in a rush of green air

dear idiotic Cora do I have to spell it out for you

you look me in the eye like a very early Kandinsky

is that a scar or a drop of Kölsch on the white rock maple

cruising on earth Cardiff singer of the world
I beg you moving slowly on down but no
problem I fall into bed & dream of Silvia Ziranek

On Romsey Rec

they call it red the sky but then
the air is always calling someone's name
the voice of Springsteen
drifting from a 1000 radios

residue of a more transparent sound
a small cloud in the sun a half-brick sailing by
flares in the dark over Cavendish Road
today & tomorrow Saint Barnabas Road

you can rest on the bench near the bowling green
& later go back by the old orphans' home
& drink from the glass the hammer the sickle
so carefully chased Jim Peck made that for me

lair before home
except after tea

Eugène Boudin

you abandon us
to swim in that full sky
to arrive at a fondness for cloud

the mass of their suspense
is moving from the depth of grey
to make it clear how blue the haze

Nijinsky

They look at you as though there were something
you didn't know something about the eyes
a look very much like my eldest daughter
at the age of one. It was during the war.
How much a face changes in the course of a day
it was as if I had become unrecognizable to you
for an instant. But later you failed to recognize me
for longer periods & fear leapt into the night
on peasant ankles leaving a long streak of lust & terror
in its wake. We take your word for it.

Sleep

you came to me in a dream in your mini-crini
turning away the crease at the top of your thighs
fickle as corduroy clean as your hair
feeling like air from another planet the new bed linen
where my heart is soothed by a breath of light
a scent of comfort on a Sunday morning
here in this your poem & mine. I beg you to free this boy.

Stacking

A little benzedrine to clear the airways
night gathers itself towards the dawn
the stars zap through my room again

the head was of some importance in all this
though sometimes I think I'm just another little bit
of River Avon driftwood well who isn't?

You are called Michael who is like God
a big sulking bruiser like yourself
o dark lovely phantom we wake again in our separate nations

Song

a breath of clean air
reaches out of the cloud
releasing particles of grit

your gaze was my undoing

                              felicity

you are stronger than me
making me do whatever you want
in the blink of an eye

Kinderlieder (1992)

After Thomas Hood

1

I remember I remember 99 Marion Street, the little rear window facing into a high brick wall at the back of Splott Road. The sun it never seemed to come into it much but there was plenty of black dust which gathered on the window-sills & took my mother's breath away at night. I think I used to have a swing, it broke my air-gun.

2

I read faster & faster at the little library just around the corner in Hinton Street where I also used to go for tea with Nana & Pop. First all of Arthur Ransome then M. Pardoe. These were chosen for me. I used to think the Lakes were some sort of Paradise that never existed. I've still only been there once & never actually saw a lake. I eventually got bored at an early age with novels about people like that who lived in exotic places. Later Nana & Pop moved in with us again when we got broke.

3

But that was, I remember, in Fairwater, with Auntie Maggie too, my Godmother. She helped to give me this endless craving. Every Wednesday afternoon at the Shaftesbury in Pompey & later at the Globe, back home in Cardiff. In the close company of the living-room, all draughts excluded for the winter, reeling under the influence of Woodbine coal & Navy Cut.

4

I remember Arabella Street but that was much earlier & Keppoch Street where we lived with my great-grandmother, looking up at her, stood on the stairs in her dark dress & long black sleeves, while I played at making the dinner with my tin gas-stove. It had sharp edges. That was the first thing I ever remember. The salt & vinegar man used to call with a horse & cart. It was flat & had rubber tyres. The vinegar was in wooden barrels & the salt in slabs. He cut it with a saw.

Sketches of a Day

1

water from the afternoon rain
ripples down the
laneside & air
breathes through
the valley
detailed in
sunlight

a passing wheel has
pressed a rat to
the tarmac

rooks
        scatter over
the tip

no one about
the sewage farm as
usual the
long-armed sprinklers
rotate above
the filter-tanks &

from the stile the
                right of way
straggles upward

the pasture all
burst with molehills

2

Fugue
    tranquillo

key
after key

touched
    hesitation

on the old cottage piano

while out the window
two elderly ladies
in straw hats
fitted jackets &
crape dresses
slack over
thin calves

step by

the hedgerow
    stippled with white
cow parsley

3

lamplight ascending through
masses of hand-shaped leaves

yellows
now some
now other pale
undersides
as they turn
in the current of air

in which the tree's spread wavers
like a reflection
on disturbed water

Song

the wind in the trees
seemed to murmur Louise
& her name was a wonderful gesture

the bump on her head
seemed to indicate Fred
& her breast used to droop when I pressed her

Israel

with Andrew Crozier

Damned sand. Sable. A fine toothy
tiger. Gritty sandwich on the beach
and salt on the skin. The sea is
dead. Yes, picnic by the dead sea. But the land is
holy. Bigger. And better. They comb out
the hills: refugees, snipers, guerilla bands and
pan-arab nationalists. All camels
have fleas, and sometimes ferrets too. To be saved.
They assure us so. And maybe little bullet
holes and marks. And griffins, hosts of
narks and angels, griffins, harpies, doves and
things to say Hello to. Or Goodbye. We walk
on the far side of the dyspeptic
strand, hunting the gritty tiger.
There the beach roves with the wettest waves
and little lost gazelles
plunder the acrylic caves and shell
ac pots. The ground holds wealth and nature
runs around, oblivious on top
of all of it, as often as not. Tea can be
served under the stuffed heads on my
study wall, the tray the harpy
carries to the beach is red with the shot
blood of my skinned silk and heralded by
the double crack that tells us
nature now lies dead, the bloodied feathers
in the brake. Of all those pleadings
in the hall, the smallest leaks away now,
a little serried rudiment, under the drooping
beach umbrellas, a little steady nutriment
to warm us now the relative is lost . . .
Please I to know your will O
Lord and grant that I may live but to do

Thy holy wish, that I may lie under
the trays at five o'clock when these are
taken quite back in.

Anglo-Irish Relations

Sefton

Shergar

Mason

Anglo-Irish Relations (Slight Return)

Sefton

Shergar

Queenie

Confession

I throw myself on a
eating utensil a nail

a tin of lemonade
my head against a wall
& smash a window

no one had asked me to do this

That Old Piano

there's a bumpy little funny little melody
you can dig down by the dock
who can tell if the sky is lying
for the gulls & the sun & the sparkling hock

she was a native starter
a definite topical hit
but she never took away oh fragrant slender
the hidden star she left me in a pit

(refrain)

she lives on just cokynuts
& fish for her tea
with a kink in her hair
& an elegant brow
& a switch in her vein for me

The Consciousness Raisers

they meet on Fridays when
the women home from the factories & the offices
& on Sunday afternoons

At night they lie in bed
& hold hands
counting the stars

From the Welsh

a crispy leaf
torn away in air

old already
born this year

Colonial Medley

valse moderato espressivo

the Wicklow hills are very hard
but to walk there again

before the young day shades to mist
the shining cliffs of Glenmalur

there's a tear in your eye
that should never be there at all

at all the power in your smile
the stones jump up beguiled

& if you go there's scarce a face
in these low lands that partly seems my own

when all is left a single chord
to break at night

oh sing sad harp
this sing for me

poverty

I used to think whenever my mother
called me Silent O'Moyle
he must have been a Newtown man

then I encounter Thomas Moore

New Road East

the amice the alb & the radio

Paul Robeson singing
Macushla Macushla

her white arms are reaching

catechism

penniless
for land or kine

I called on Napper Tandy
beside a ghostly barrow

the pale moon rose
above the shining wave

he sd
it wasn't like 1916 in 1916 either

mixed marriage medley

out of the sleeping west
that dangerous gap

came a dark bandage
it sd

discourse the darling
in sunshine or in shadow

but when you kiss
you're one of nothing

the little shirt me mother made for me

Danny

a little bit of shrapnel fell
from out the sky one day

the call to foreign parts
he'd thought to follow

it sd if your name is
Timothy

then I'm green turning red
over you

Grace

God bless us & save us
sys Anthony Davies

I never knew bloaters was fish

Gnome

the life of oysters
& the life of Reilly
are not to be compared

Skip

Monday come
Tuesday go

Wednesday reap
Thursday sow

Friday swim

Saturday
Sunday

well
certainly

Skip

o Jocasta keep my arm in plaster

Gender

Denise is a very secretive people & so am I

The American President Addresses West Berlin

i am a doughnut

January 1983

1

I gotta trial for the Yankees

2

you know what I mean by the Yankees

3

Yankees go home you mean

4

they never really made us Yankees

The Sandwich

Terrible Attacks of

Invisibility on King's Parade

Late Twentieth Century Britain &

The Invisible Man Returns

I'd almost forgotten how to relax

I suppose I'll get used to this

1. thumb

2. index-finger

the new blood itself was the antidote

The Bee Code of Hywel Dda

The worth of an old colony is twenty-four pence

The worth of the first swarm sixteen pence

The worth of the bull-swarm twelve pence

The third swarm is worth eight pence

The first swarm to come from the primary swarm is worth
    twelve pence

The first swarm to come from the bull-swarm eight pence

The first swarm to come from the third swarm is worth four new
    pence
& it should not swarm until after the first of August
& it is called a wing-swarm

The worth of the mother of a hive of bees: it is worth twenty-four
    pence
& so they bide until the first of November

From the first of November onwards each one is an old colony &
    is worth twenty-four pence except for the wing-swarm:
it is not an old colony until the first of May
for it is not known till then if it will live

Schlegel Eats a Bagel (1996)

February

Schubert spoke to me in the bath
it came through a hole in the wall the light
shone through the trees
& took away our grief
in saecula saeculorum amen

Retro

bereft of you for no good reason
I can understand
& haunted by my mind
I scan the optics

reading upside down
like everyone else
in the 50s

Poem

1

this cat is wearing a noisy coat
we slay him for his pain

2

in the late night
supermarket
of my knee

there creeps a
quiet little
cuddly bee

3

art is a balm to the brain
& gives a certain resolution

Blue Scar Watch

una smarrita vittima/ di ossesse speranze
PIER PAOLO PASOLINI

a single rowan
at the edge

of the forest
on the ridge

bare hardship
long night

slippery path
& swirling air

1

Rowena of the long red hair
stay for the amber light

no veteran
was a weakling in youth

but I won't deny
I'm sick tonight

for the paradise
of sunlit oak

ah little pen
it's deep midwinter

2

my mother told me
that I am your son

& long as you are dead
I do lament you

but if you are safe
I will see you again

despite the horror
at sea

your grave is faultless & good
beside the river

& I am penniless
in England

3

o little pear tree
I did not eat shit like a dog

every hectare
gone to the reaver

it's better to strike
than supplicate

the starlings chatter
my heart is raw

4

carry the head
to the white crest

of Striding Edge
above Red Tarn

from the east
to the north

they went west
& I remain

5

little wooden leaf
supporting spray

the lark will sing
on Pen-y-Fan

caught as we are
below the city

6

a patrician head
of golden hair

Michael has the cattle
in the byre

& whiskey
in the bowl

but the rain is fierce
over here

at the head of the valley
the pits are drowning

7

walk on the wild wet shingle
where the bright wave

in one expansive movement
flings love & foam

into the grey &
silver matrix

8

at the mouth of the Severn
a shining wave flows out

Sabrina fair a boy
who loved you

would love you again
au printemps

9

the lake is cold
under a stormy sky

brittle reeds
& broken branches

trees bend
toward evening

it will soon be spring
little pen

10

a dish of calf's liver
drinking red wine

a clear glass vessel
to ease a warrior

stay until Sunday
little one

with the cuckoo
comes the summer

Rune

begin again
beside
the lough

a stone
a pen
to draw

the tip
across
the nail

the shaft
a blade
apart

to spread
a dorsal
fin

as far
& wide
a sail

a nib
agility
by name

Idyl

tiny fish
start from her knee

just below
the amber glow

of lapping sea
in Brittany

another year of heavy dreams
the smell of slurry everywhere

a potato farl a cup of tea
too hot to sip

a drifting film of yellow sky
cold in the north

a sudden ease
driv in the vein

inches of soda bread
adorn the plate

the farmer's son goes off to perform
in the milking parlour

later we dispatch another bull
in father's honour

each with a glass or two
before the night

whiskey & water & a small cigar
echo echo

[364]

"hello boys
it's me again

I come to greet you
far & when

the horizon opens like a door
the speed of light is not a possible speed

for a person cannot overtake light
what can never be reached so

heart break tomorrow
it ain't always sorrow

the line knows where it's going
& we know we're going with it

I leave the rest to you
distance no object

Printed in the United Kingdom
by Lightning Source UK Ltd.
121772UK00002B/159/A

PUBLISHED BY SALT PUBLISHING
PO Box 202, Applecross, Western Australia 6153
PO Box 937, Great Wilbraham, Cambridge PDO CB1 5JX United Kingdom

© John James, 2002

The right of John James to be identified as the
author of this work has been asserted by him in accordance
with Section 77 of the Copyright, Designs and Patents Act 1988.

First published 2002

Printed and bound in the United Kingdom by Lightning Source

Typeset in Swift 9.5 / 13

ISBN 1 876857 40 4 paperback

SP

1 3 5 7 9 8 6 4 2

Collected Poems

JOHN JAMES

SALT

Collected Poems

JOHN JAMES was born in 1939 in Cardiff and educated by the De La Salle Brothers at Saint Illtyd's College there. He left in 1957 to read Philosophy and English Literature at the University of Bristol and later undertook postgraduate studies in American Literature at the University of Keele. He was a founder of *The Resuscitator* in Bristol in 1963 and Arts Council Creative Writing Fellow, University of Sussex, 1978–79. He is Head of Communication Studies at Anglia Polytechnic University, Cambridge.